Fascinating Women In California History

By Alton Pryor

Fascinating Women In California History

By Alton Pryor

Fascinating Women In California History

Copyright © 2003 by Alton Pryor

ISBN: 0-9660053-9-2
Library of Congress Control Number: 2003090424

First Printing 2003
Second Printing 2003
Third Printing 2003
Fourth Printing 2005

Stagecoach Publishing
5360 Campcreek Loop
Roseville, CA 95747
Phone (916) 771-8166
Email: stagecoach@surewest.net
www.stagecoachpublishing.com

"Remember the Ladies, and be more generous and favorable to them than your ancestors."

"Do not put such unlimited power into the hands of the husbands. Remember all men would be tyrants if they could."

(Quotes by Abigail Adams, wife of John Adams, second President of the United States.)

Table of Contents

1

The Sisters of Mercy

Mother Frances Bridgerman, superior of the Sisters of Mercy in Kinsale, Ireland, had a problem. When a priest asked Mother Frances to select recruits to go to San Francisco in 1854, she hesitated, fearing the women would get scalped.

Mother Mary Baptist Russell

Despite San Francisco's reputation as a lawless city, twenty-nine Irish Sisters of Mercy volunteered to serve there. From that group, Mother Frances chose eight. She selected 26-year-old Sr. Mary Baptist Russell as the group's leader.

Thus, from the Irish seaport town of Kinsale in 1854 came eight young women to a completely different environment, one that was populated with gold prospectors, fortune hunters, and opportunists. When the Sisters of Mercy arrived in San Francisco December 8, 1854, what they found was jarring.

"Gold fever" had hit the men, and many had left their wives and children to fend for themselves while they went off to pursue their fortunes.

The exploitation and sale of women were common practices in the roaring city, and the aged and infirm fared little better.

Mother Mary Baptist Russell was determined to help the suffering. One of her first activities was to create a safe haven for women. Under her leadership, the Sisters of Mercy began taking in abandoned wives and mothers, prostitutes, and naïve young girls. They also took in the elderly and began visiting the sick in their homes.

Less than a month after their arrival, the sisters were asked to visit a woman who had just died. "While kneeling to pray for the woman," said author Sr. Mary Katherine Doyle, "They realized she was not dead." After sending for the priest, they revived the woman and sent her to the county hospital.

Mary Baptist deliberately rented a house near the hospital. Daily the sisters visited the sick, intent on bringing what comfort they could to the patients. "At that time, people who went into the hospital rarely left alive," author Doyle wrote.

"They were left all night in the dark with no water and no one attending them. They had no linen or pillows—they were expected to bring their own if they had any. The nurses there (in the hospital) were people who were not employable anywhere else."

When the 1855 cholera outbreak struck San Francisco, the Sisters of Mercy themselves went to work as nurses in the county hospital.

The San Francisco *Daily News* described the sisters' labors during the health crisis:

"A more horrible and ghastly sight we have seldom witnessed. In the midst of this scene of sorrow, pain, anguish, and danger were ministering angels who disregarded everything to aid their distressed fellow creatures. The Sisters of Mercy did not stop to inquire whether the poor sufferers were Protestants or Catholics, Americans or foreigners, but with the noblest devotion applied themselves to their relief."

The cholera disease ultimately killed about five percent of the population.

While Mother Russell's most significant contributions were medical, it was ironic in that she had absolutely no formal medical training. Still, according to the San Francisco Examiner, more than any other single individual, she helped California emerge from the dark ages of hospital care.

Because of their effectiveness during the cholera epidemic, the sisters were asked to take charge of the county hospital. Mother Baptist agreed, but after months of caring for the indigent at the sisters' expense, she told the county it would have to meet its financial obligation to the sisters.

She ended up buying the hospital for $14,000, and when the county built a new hospital, Mother Baptist opened Saint Mary's in 1857, the first Catholic Hospital on the West Coast.

Baptist Russell apparently didn't plan ahead on what she was going to do. She simply experienced reality and then began to build. For instance, she had not planned to build a home for the aged, but when someone came and asked for shelter and there was no place to put her, she began her project for sheltering the infirm aged.

She relied heavily on the providence of God, and often began a project without funding. This prompted one bishop to comment, "Her heart was bigger than her purse."

In 1868, the city was besieged with a different disease outbreak. Smallpox hit the city. The disease was so contagious that even ministers would not visit their dying parishioners.

City officials opened pest houses for those inflicted with the disease. Nurses worked only during the day, leaving victims of smallpox unattended in the darkness from dusk until dawn.

Sr. Mary Baptist asked for and received permission for the sisters to work in the pest houses. For ten months the sisters lived among the smallpox victims.

Mother Baptist worked with atheists, agnostics, bigots, criminals, murderers, as well as those more upstanding. One writer said, "She loved to help people—especially the poor—and in so doing, she became a legend.

She provided wedding dresses for brides too poor to purchase them. She visited men in prisons. She stole from the hospital linen supply to give to the poor. Legend has it that Mother Baptist would pull up her petticoat and wrap the hospital bed linens around her waist and stuff them in her sleeves.

When she reached the home of a needy family, she would pull the linen out and make the beds. She did this so often that the sisters put locks on the linen closets. One time, she pulled her own mattress down the stairs to give it to a poor man.

As good as her works were, she and her Sisters of Mercy had their detractors. An anti-catholic writer accused the Sisters of mismanaging the hospital and of abusing the patients. In her direct way of getting to the issue, Mother Baptist urged a grand jury investigation into the allegations of the accuser.

The grand jury lauded the hospital as one of three outstanding institutions of San Francisco, along with the schools and the fire department.

Mother Baptist Russell died in August 1898, and thousands came to her funeral. Fr. R.E. Kenna, a Jesuit priest, summed up her life in a letter to the bereaved sisters:

"Gentle as a little child, she was brave and resolute as a crusader. Prudence itself, yet she was fearless in doing good to the needy...all who met her were forced to admire; and those who knew her best loved her most."

(Author's note: Much of this material was first published in the book, "A Call to Care: The Women Who Built Catholic Healthcare in America." The book is now out of print.)

The Sisters of Mercy Convent in Grass Valley is part of St. Patrick's Church built there in 1858. The Henry Scadden house on the right was first used as an orphanage for small boys and later as a Sisters Chapel.

School Established in Grass Valley

(Paraphrased from "The Story of Mount Saint Mary's)

In the spring of 1862 Father Thomas J. Dalton, pastor of the thriving community of Grass Valley, applied to the Sisters of Mercy at Saint Mary's Hospital in San Francisco for the founding of a branch house of their order in Grass Valley.

The first request was turned down on the grounds that there were not enough sisters available. Father Dalton was persistent. In August, he convinced Mother Mary Baptist Russell to make the trip to Grass Valley to judge if it was a place suitable for a house of their order. She did so, accompanied by Sister M. Paul Beechinor and Sister M. Teresa King.

She was immediately surprised by what she saw. A beautiful new brick church had been built and opened on December 5, 1859. It was modeled on the Irish school system.

Mother M. Baptist Russell returned to San Francisco and wrote to Bishop Eugene O'Connell, Vicar Apostolic of Marysville, in whose territory Grass Valley was located.

Several letters were exchanged between the two religious figures, and along with great persuasion from Father Dalton, Mother Baptist Russell agreed to bring a branch of her order to Grass Valley.

The Sisters of Mercy ran the school from 1863 until 1986, when the parish purchased it. It is the oldest Catholic school in continuous operation in California.

Chapter 2

Donaldina Cameron

She rescued Chinese slave girls

Donaldina Cameron was brought to the Presbyterian Mission Home in San Francisco in 1895 to teach sewing to Asian girls and women.

Donaldina Cameron

Most of these women were brought to California as slaves. Some were as young as six years of age when the mission rescued them.

They were usually kidnapped, but just as frequently, they were sold by their parents in China, and forced to work as domestics and prostitutes in the United States. Shortly after Donaldina arrived, her supervisor died. This threw Donaldina, who was twenty-five years old, into the position of director.

She is credited with saving more than three thousand women and children during her forty-seven years at the mission. To those she rescued, she was known as *"White Angel"* and as *"Lo Mo"*, which means Beloved Mother.

Slave dealers and brothel owners did not hold her in such esteem. To them she was *"White Devil"*.

Often the rescues consisted only of Donaldina and a companion. They would simply walk past the Chinese guards and escort the girls back to the mission. The guards were usually so confused and surprised at the sight of a white woman in the Chinese ghetto that they turned and ran.

Once safely in the mission, Donaldina and other missionaries helped to give the girls a better life. They were taught English and perhaps reading and writing—according to their situations. The girls were also introduced to Christianity and the Bible, as well as cooking, cleaning and sewing.

Many of these women were smuggled into the United States, circumventing immigration laws that excluded them. They were simply commodities that were bought and sold as property. The system was known as the *"yellow slave trade."*

Bogus contracts were created to keep the system working. The contracts were written with insurmountable conditions, making it impossible for the women to purchase their own freedom. Some say the number of Asian women who died in enslaved conditions in San Francisco numbered in the thousands.

Gaining entry into the United States was complicated for the Chinese by the Chinese Exclusion Acts of 1882, 1888, 1892, and 1902 and the Immigration Act of 1924.

These acts increased restrictions on Asian immigrants, especially laborers. Only students, teachers or merchants were admitted to America. The acts were clearly discriminatory, as no other national group was denied entry to the country.

According to Paul Q. Chow, who wrote a thesis on the subject, the fear was that laborers from China would take jobs away from European-American workers. This fear was made worse because of the severe economic depression facing the country at that time.

When Donaldina Cameron, a New Zealand-born Scot, arrived in San Francisco from the San Joaquin Valley, her intention was to devote a "single year" working in the Chinese Presbyterian Mission at 920 Sacramento Street.

When she became aware of the slavery and conditions in Chinatown, she felt repulsed. From a mild-mannered missionary girl, Donaldina was transformed into a zealous social reformer. She became fanatically committed to wiping out the horrors of yellow slavery.

A San Francisco Examiner article by Michael Svanevik and Shirley Burgett detailed the lengths to which Cameron would go. "Slavery, was a fact of life in China," they wrote. "For centuries, young girls were taught to think of themselves as creatures almost purely for the enjoyment of men and were sold as merchandize to be wives, concubines or prostitutes."

Most of those arriving in California during the gold rush were sold for immoral purposes. State officials were bought off by the Chinese slavers and refused to recognize the existence of the slavery practice.

Most of the girls in San Francisco's Chinatown worked in cribs—narrow cells that accommodated two to six girls. They were required to service all comers, most of whom were white. Patrons paid twenty five to fifty cents for sexual services. Young boys were admitted for fifteen cents.

According to the San Francisco Examiner, The Presbyterian Mission spearheaded reform against the yellow slave trade as early as the 1870s. Margaret Culbertson, then the mission's director, instituted raids to liberate captive children.

Donaldina Cameron became Culbertson's assistant in 1895 and assumed the directorship two years later on Culbertson's death.

Cameron became the scourge of the underworld, the Examiner wrote. "She came to know every back alley and rooftop in Chinatown. She undertook rescues of young captives who requested assistance or when maltreatment of a child was reported.

When denied access to a crib or parlor, she relied on an unofficial alliance she had developed with San Francisco Police Sergeant Jack Manion, commander of the so-called Chinatown Squad. Manion sympathized with Cameron and ordered his men to "give her whatever she wants."

Police officers in plain clothes gained entry where Cameron could not. They simply pounded down doors with sledgehammers, crowbars and axes.

Plans for such raids were generally kept very secret, but word of them sometimes leaked out and the girls were herded into passageways, tunnels or secret rooms.

The San Francisco Examiner noted that Cameron did not limit her activities to San Francisco. She led raids in virtually every city on the Pacific Coast. She admitted that she often found it necessary to "break the letter though not the spirit of the law."

Not all girls came to the mission willingly. Many became so frightened at the appearance of Cameron that they jeopardized their own rescues, the Examiner report said. At least some were forced into the mission against their will.

"The activities of Cameron and the Presbyterians endangered a very lucrative operation," the Examiner reporters explained. "Slave girls represented big money both for the brokers who imported them and for corrupt officials who looked the other way."

During the 1850s, girls sold for between $100 and $500. By the end of World War I, prices had risen to as high as $7,000. Yellow slavery flourished until the 1930s.

The slavery overlords expressed their displeasure with Cameron's crusade. On one occasion, a dynamite bomb was found on the steps of 920 Sacramento Street and disarmed without any damage.

The mission also opened its doors to girls such as Tye Leung, who was born in the United States. Tye lived in a two-room apartment in Chinatown with her mother, father, six brothers and one sister.

Tye's parents had arrived before the Chinese Exclusion Acts were enacted. Tye's parents had allowed her and her brothers and a sister to adapt American ways. The girls even attended school.

Yet, the father and mother clung to some of their Chinese culture. They selected a bridegroom for their daughter. Tye firmly rejected the idea that she would marry the man her parents had chosen for her. He was a complete stranger to her and wanted to cart her off to Butte, Montana, a place she knew absolutely nothing about.

Rather than go through with such a marriage, Tye secretly left the home of her mother and father and sought asylum in Donaldina Cameron's mission.

Donaldina Cameron retired in 1938 after forty-seven years with the mission. Four years later, the mission was renamed the Cameron House in her honor. Donaldina Cameron died in 1968 at the age of ninety-eight.

Chapter 3

Dorothea Lange

Her Work Made A Difference

Dorothea Lange was not one of California's earliest women pioneers, but she was one of its most important. New York Times critic A.D. Coleman called Lange's photographs "documents of such a high order that they convey the feelings of the victims as well as the facts of the crime." Her most notable photograph was called simply, "Migrant Mother," depicting a destitute farm worker in the pea fields of Nipomo, California.

Dorothea Lange on photo shoot.

Here is Lange's own account of how she came to shoot the picture while traveling through the vegetable fields of Santa Barbara County.

"I saw and approached a hungry and desperate mother, as if drawn by a magnet. I do not remember how I explained my presence or my camera to her, but I do remember she asked me no questions. I made five exposures, working closer and closer from the same direction.

"I did not ask her name or her history. She told me her age, that she was thirty-two. She said that they were living on frozen vegetables from the surrounding fields, and on birds that the children killed.

"She had just sold the tires from her car to buy food. There she sat in that lean-to tent with her children huddled around her, and seemed to know that my pictures might help her, and so she helped me. There was a sort of equality about it."

Dorothea continued, "I was following instinct, not reason. I drove into that wet and soggy camp and parked my car like a homing pigeon."

When she returned to her home in Berkeley, Dorothea developed the film. When she saw what she had, she rushed the photographs to the San Francisco News' editor.

The newspaper reported the story, along with Dorothea's photographs, of the 2,500 migrant workers, who, like the young mother in her photograph, were stranded and hungry because of crop failure.

The federal government responded to the story with 20,000 pounds of food.

When Dorothea was twelve years old, her father Henry Nutzhorn, abandoned her family, leaving her mother, Joan Lange Nutzhorn, Dorothea and her young brother, Martin, alone. She never saw her father again and rarely ever spoke of him.

Joan, who worked as a librarian to support herself and her two children, moved in with her mother, Sophie Vottler Lange, who lived in Hoboken.

26

Migrant Woman
(Dorothea Lange Collection, Oakland Museum)

Dorothea may have gained her artistic eye from her grandmother, who was an expert dressmaker and always sought perfection.

Sophie once told Dorothea, "Of all the things beautiful in the world, there is nothing finer than the orange." Dorothea knew what she meant.

Each day, Dorothea would travel with her mother from Hoboken to Manhattan, where her mother worked at the New York branch library. Dorothea attended nearby Public School 62.

Dorothea didn't like school, and was prone to playing hooky when she attended high school. Despite missing so many classes, she did graduate Wadleigh High School.

When her mother asked her what she would now do since she had graduated, she promptly answered that she wanted to be a photographer, even though she had no camera and had never made a photograph.

To please her mother, she enrolled in the New York Training School for Teachers. It was while walking down Fifth Avenue one day that she noticed a fine collection of portrait photographs in a display window.

She went inside and persuaded Arnold Genthe, to hire her as an apprentice. She later learned that he was quite a famous photographer.

Dorothea worked in Genthe's Studio each day after school for fifteen dollars a week, printing proofs of film which Genthe had shot, and she carefully "spotted" negatives that showed white spots as a result of dust on the film. She learned to mount and frame finished photographs.

Genthe appreciated Dorothea's work. To show his appreciation, he gave her a camera.

Assured that photography was her future, Dorothea then worked as an apprentice in a number of shops, learning to operate the big 8 x 10 Graphic cameras.

One day, the studio owner at which she worked gave Dorothea a new assignment. The shop's professional portrait photographer had quit, and Mrs. Beatty, the shop owner, needed someone to photograph the wealthy Brokaw family. Dorothea's outstanding photographs launched her on a career as a portrait photographer.

The budding photographer then took a course in photography at Columbia University. She used a chicken coop in the backyard of her family's home to set up a darkroom. Her photography earnings helped support the family.

When she was twenty-two years old, Dorothea and her closest friend, Fronsie Ahlstrom decided to tour the world. With $140 in cash, they set out, traveling from New York to New Orleans by boat. They took a train west, stopping in Texas and New Mexico, and finally landed in San Francisco.

Fronsie took a job with Western Union, and Dorothea landed a job in the photo-finishing department of a department and dry goods store named "Marsh and Company."

A friend later financed a portrait studio for Dorothea at 540 Sutter Street in San Francisco. She soon became one of the city's most popular portrait photographers, especially among city officials.

She met and married Maynard Dixon, a painter of Western wilderness scenes, on March 21, 1920. During the next few years, Dorothea traveled with her husband when he went on sketching trips.

Dorothea's true mission in life came to her during a brewing thunderstorm. "When it broke, there I was, sitting on a big rock—right in the middle of it, with the thunder bursting and the wind whistling, it came to me that what I had to do was to take pictures and concentrate upon people, only people, all kinds of people, people who paid me and people who didn't."

She found that photographing people outside her studio was different from the crafted poses she could devise in her studio. Now she was forced to accept her subjects in their general surroundings.

This experience was adding to her development as a social observer. One of her first photos on her new-found mission was photographing the White Angel Breadline in San Francisco.

This photo was destined to become one of the most lasting images of the Depression era. The photo focuses on an unshaven old man, leaning on a rail with a tin cup while awaiting a free meal at a bread line.

Lange then formed an alliance with Paul Taylor, a university economics professor and writer of contemporary events. Together, Lange and Taylor looked at the struggles of the migrant workers brought to California and paid low wages for hard work.

Taylor wrote about these living conditions, and Dorothea photographed them. Their reports were so strong that California responded by building camps where migrant families could live.

Lange and her husband Maynard Dixon had grown apart, and finally divorced. Lange then married Paul Taylor in December 1935.

For the next thirty years they continued working together documenting events of the times.

Dorthea Lange's "White Angel Breadline" photograph, shot in San Francisco in 1933, was destined to become one of the lasting images of the Depression era. (Oakland Museum)

(Author's note: Dorothea Lange died October 11, 1965, at age seventy.)

Noted photographer Willard Van Dyke said of Dorothea, "She tried to keep her mind open like a roll of sensitive, unexposed film."

Chapter 4

The Ladies of the Evening

There was no lack of customers

Women were so few in number in San Francisco in1848 that word of one passing by in the street would quickly empty a saloon of its inhabitants. Some estimates put the number of females arriving in San Francisco during 1848 at less than 100. Some of the ships from Chile and Peru arriving in San Francisco carried women that were often not wives, widows, nor maids.

Sally Stanford

Most of the men and families came overland, while those women intending to engage in prostitution came by ship, from Mazatlan, Guaymas, or San Blas. Few, if any, had money for passage. Spanish-Californian Captain Jose Fernandez explained, "They did not pay passage on the ships. When they reached San Francisco, the captains sold them to the highest bidder."

When any ship arrived from a Mexican port, there were men who took two or three small boats or a launch out to meet the ship. They boarded the ship, paid the passages for ten to twelve of the women without their own passage money.

The women were then taken immediately to cantinas, where the newcomers were forced to prostitute themselves for half a year, during which the proprietors took the bulk of their earnings.

Little has been written about these so-called women of the night, but Curt Gentry did tackle the subject in his 1964 book, The Madams of San Francisco."

According to Gentry, "Almost all of those arriving were of Mexican, Spanish, or French descent. Most came from Mexico, Central, and South America. From early 1849 through at least 1852, these areas were to provide more of California's prostitutes (and dance-hall girls) than all other countries combined."

One writer, William S. McCollum, in his book, "California As I saw It", carried a dim view of the women prostitutes as a whole. "The Senoritas are not fascinating, because they are not pretty—they are very willing to be gazed at, however, and are inclined to co-quetry. I must confess I prefer something lighter—and less greasy—more graceful and less indolent, and above all, something which can speak English."

Mark Twain once wrote the following about the Nicaraguan women that had landed in San Francisco,

"They are virtuous, according to their lights, but I guess that their lights are a little dim."

One author painted an even more distasteful picture of the women from Paraguay. "Everybody smokes in Paraguay, and nearly every female above thirteen years of age chews. Only imagine yourself about to kiss a magnificent little Hebe, arrayed in satin and flashing with diamonds; she puts you back with one delicate hand, while with the fair, tapered fingers of the other she draws forth from her mouth a brownish-black roll of tobacco, quite two inches long and looking like a monstrous grub, and deposits the delicate morsel on the rim of your sombrero, puts up her face and is ready for a salute!"

In that period, with so few females in California, wrote one Sacramento woman," Every man thought every woman in that day a beauty. Even I have had men come forty miles over the mountains, just to look at me, and I never was called a handsome woman in my best day even by my most ardent admirers."

No California madam was quite as famous as Sally Stanford who maintained perhaps the classiest houses in San Francisco during the 1930s. Her house became so famous a landmark that it was included on the city's sightseeing tours.

Sally Stanford was born Mabel Janice Busby. She changed her name while walking down Kearney Street one day and saw a newspaper headline, "Stanford Wins Big Game".

"That's for me!" she told herself. "I'm going after big game."

A story is told about a young policeman, bursting into her establishment and announcing, "I'm bustin' this place!"

"Before you do that buster," Sally coolly told him, "I suggest you go out to the kitchen and talk to your dad—we were just having a cup of coffee."

New York's famous madam, Polly Adler, once visited Sally. Adler told Sally, "You know the madam's lament—everybody goes upstairs but us."

After police closed her down in 1949, Sally opened the Valhalla restaurant in Sausalito. She later was elected to the City Council and even served as mayor of the town.

One of San Francisco's earliest businesswomen was Ah Toy, said to be the city's first Chinese prostitute.

Ah Toy was different from the other Chinese women plying their trade. Curt Gentry, in his "Madams of San Francisco, explained, "The Chinese prostitutes were usually short; Ah Toy was tall. They were usually "big-foot" peasant women; Ah Toy had aristocratic "lily-bound" feet."

It was in February 1848 that two men and one woman reached San Francisco aboard the brig Eagle. Soon after, perhaps in early 1849, a second Chinese woman arrived. The first woman to arrive had been a servant. The second woman was Ah Toy, a twenty-year-old prostitute.

Ah Toy's first residence was a small one-room shanty down an alley off Clay Street. It was located just above Kearny, in what soon became San Francisco's Chinatown.

According to Gentry in his *Madams of San Francisco*, "The line of men outside Ah Toy's shack was sometimes a block long. Chroniclers say that whenever a boat from Sacramento docked, the miners would break into a run for Ah Toy's."

Soon, there was a disruption in Ah Toy's life. Leaders in the Chinese community received a letter from a Hong Kong man claiming to be Ah Toy's legal husband. He wanted her returned."

She denied being married to the man. She testified in court that her name was Miss Ah Toy. She further said in court that she was twenty-one-years old, had been born in Canton, and had sailed to San Francisco to "better her condition." She asked the judge to allow her to stay in California. He so ruled.

Apparently satisfied and pleased with California's justice system, Ah Toy later instigated an action of her own. She complained that some of the miners had been defrauding her.

When they paid her fee of one ounce of gold ($16), which she weighed on her own scale, she was getting brass filings instead of gold.

She proceeded to point out some of the guilty miners that were sitting in court at the time. Everyone in court guffawed. The judge asked her for proof. Her evidence didn't satisfy the judge and the case was dismissed.

Some accounts say she thereafter limited her clientele to Chinese men.

There were some that claimed the Chinese prostitutes in San Francisco were responsible for the high rate of syphilis that kept the hospitals filled.

Historian Charles Caldwell Dobie found this accusation could not be true, inasmuch as by the end of 1851, the total of Chinese women in the city numbered only about seven. The number of prostitutes from other races plying their trade in San Francisco at the same time was well over one thousand.

Ah Toy reportedly died in San Jose, according to a February 2, 1928 issue of the San Francisco Examiner. She died within a few days of her 100th birthday.

Another of the gold camps' most memorable ladies was the elegant Eleanor Dumont. When she stepped down from the stage in Nevada City in 1854, all heads, both men and women, turned in her direction.

She appeared to be in her early twenties and her activities mystified residents of the mining town for days. She was neatly and stylishly dressed, and looked fresh even after her grueling stage ride.

Miners couldn't help but cast admiring glances at this classy-appearing lady. They couldn't figure out what a young woman like her would be doing in a rough and tumble town like Nevada City.

Some surmised the lady might be the town's new schoolteacher. Others thought she might have arrived to join a fiancée. Others thought even worse, that she might be a madam or looking for such a person for whom to work.

Two young miners readily agreed to carry her bags into Fepp's Hotel where she registered as "Eleanora Dumont".

For days the elegant Madame Eleanora Dumont wandered up and down dusty Broad Street, the main street in Nevada City, peering into windows of shops that had gone out of business. Her activity only increased the curiosity of the miners as well as that of the few wives of miners now living in the mining town.

Commented one woman, "There's got to be some bad in a girl with all her charms who seems to have nothing to do but strut up and down Main Street."

Finally, the mystery of Eleanor Dumont came out in the open. It happened when she handed a printing order to Editor Wait of the *Nevada Journal*.

"I want this handbill printed and distributed to every man in this town," she told the editor, "to let them know I am opening the best gambling emporium in northern California."

Soon after, the charming Eleanor opened "Vingt-et-Un" (French for twenty-one). It was a finely furnished and carpeted gambling saloon for only well-behaved and well-groomed men.

Madame Dumont served champagne instead of whiskey, and she dealt the cards herself. It didn't take her miner clientele long to observe that Miss Dumont knew her gambling profession well.

The smitten miners lost their hard-earned gold pokes, earned from their day in the mines, to the deft-fingered Miss Dumont. She seldom lost her deals or her demure smile as she collected the miner's gold. They seemed to think it a privilege just to be in her presence.

Unsatisfied with her club's limited gaming, Eleanor expanded her casino to include faro and chuck-a-luck. She hired more dealers and added a small band of violinists to entertain the gamblers.

As far as anyone knew, Eleanor Dumont had no lovers. She kept her personal life private.

It was during her second year in Nevada City that close observers saw the unflattering growth of hair on her upper lip. Because of this, she was given the equally unflattering name, *"Madame Moustache"*. Soon, it seemed, miners came to see the mustachioed lady as much as they did to gamble.

In time, Eleanor sold her Nevada City gambling emporium and began wandering through the gold country. She drifted throughout the mining camps of the western territories, even spending time in Deadwood, South Dakota, and in mining camps in Montana, Idaho and Nevada.

Eleanor Dumont became notorious throughout the west. One story tells about her being accosted by two drunks as she walked home one dark night.

"We'll take your purse," one growled.

"No, you'll not," she calmly informed the pair.

One of the robbers held a gun on her, telling her she had better hand over her purse, or else. She reached under her skirt as if to pull out her purse, but instead brought out a derringer.

Firing point blank, she killed one man and the other disappeared into the night.

It is said that natural aging eventually replaced the youthful charms of Eleanor Dumont. She put on weight and her once hourglass figure turned plump.

Even worse, her moustache turned even more prominent, darkening her upper lip. Her gambling skill had left her and she soon turned to prostitution.

She maintained a *"bawdy"* house in Bannock, Montana, at one time.

Some say that one of her girls in that enterprise was Martha Jane Canary, later known as *"Calamity Jane."* Eleanor then moved on to San Francisco to try her luck, but that venture failed.

At one point, she gave up her fast-paced gambling and prostitution ways and settled down on a ranch in eastern Nevada. She married a small-time gambler but made the mistake of turning over her savings to him. He squandered her money and disappeared.

The once-beautiful Eleanor Dumont eventually showed up in Bodie, the "toughest town in the west." She struggled to survive and soon became an object of pity by the townspeople.

On September 13, 1879, the Aurora, Nevada, *Esmeralda Herald* carried an obituary, noting that the body of a woman was found two miles south of Bodie and was identified as that of Eleanor Dumont, more familiarly known as *"Madame Moustache."*

Some say the gamblers and bartenders who had known Eleanor saw to it that she had a decent burial in a good cemetery, rather than in a pauper's grave.

Gold miners seemed to have a particular fascination with the French women arriving in San Francisco with the obvious intention of setting up a red-light shop.

Albert Benard, a thirty-one year old Frenchman who came to San Francisco, worked as an actor and later as a journalist for the city's first French newspaper.

His view of the French women who came to San Francisco was certainly different than that of the gold miners casting admiring glances.

"If the poor fellows had known what these women had been in Paris, how one could pick them up on the boulevards and have them for almost nothing, they might not have been as free with their offers of $500 or $600 a night," Benard wrote.

Some of the women, he said, made enough in one month in San Francisco to go home to France and live on their incomes, but many were not so lucky. "No doubt, they were blind to their own wrinkled and faded skins, and were too confident in their ability to deceive Americans regarding the dates on their birth certificates."

The first French women did not at first go to work in the brothels. Instead, they rented their own apartments. Then, from noon until midnight, they hired themselves out to gambling establishments at large salaries.

Their jobs in the establishments were simply to grace the gambling tables, giving the gamblers a little something extra to look at. After they finished work, they were able to entertain callers in their small apartments. They undoubtedly began filling their evening appointment books while still at the tables.

In their native land most of the French girls were "streetwalkers of the cheapest sort." Whatever their background, these women knew how to pleasure the women-hungry gold miners.

A miner, whether he wanted it or not, would be given a bath, a shave, and new cloths to put on before enjoying the services of the French demimondes.

The miners were grateful and willing to pay for such pleasures, however brief. It was a welcome break from the backbreaking, and too often, unrewarding work in the gold diggings.

Chapter 5

Juanita

First Woman to Be Hanged in California

In the gold town of Downieville, the Fourth of July in 1851 was an important event. About every able-bodied man in town was most certain to celebrate. Along with the big parade, the political speeches, and other patriotic fanfare, alcohol flowed in copious amounts to help liven the affair.

Downieville, in fact, was probably as well known for its two-fisted drinking as for the rich gold deposits found there. It was the metropolis of the Yuba mines by the early 1850s and gold miners grew thick along the North Fork.

The town was named for William Downie, a Scotsman that settled there when he, accompanied by an Irishman, an Indian, a Hawaiian and ten blacks, struck rich gold. They built a log cabin, but because of the inclement weather, settled down to wait out the winter before working their claim.

The group had a lofty decision to make in the winter of 1849. They had a single bottle of brandy, and had to decide whether to consume it on Christmas, or wait until the New Year.

Heated arguments ensued over the next several days, in the close environments of the log cabin. Those in favor of opening the bottle on Christmas Day finally won, probably because it would give them an earlier opportunity to celebrate.

When Christmas finally arrived, the treasured bottle of brandy was opened. It was mixed into a punch, with the addition of nutmeg and hot water.

The punch obviously had its intended effect, for at the height of the evening, Major Downie climbed to the roof of the cabin with an American flag in one hand and a pistol in the other. He made a short speech, fired into the air with his pistol, and gave three cheers for the American Constitution.

The Fourth of July, 1851, was just as wildly celebrated, as had been any previous occasion that remotely resembled an excuse to drink. But this celebration resulted in a happening that circulated around the world, making Downieville notoriously famous.

Late at night, following his Fourth of July carousing, a well-liked Australian miner named Joe Cannon reeled his way homeward with several companions. He either accidentally or purposefully fell through the doorway of a dwelling.

Inside, lived Juanita, the famed senorita of this story, and her Mexican boyfriend. Juanita was described as 23 years old, beautiful, and, some said, pregnant.

One version of the story is that Cannon returned to Juanita's house the following day. Some say it was to apologize, but others thought that lust might have been a truer motive.

A bystander claimed he heard Cannon approach Juanita and her Mexican boyfriend while they were standing in the doorway of their house. The unnamed

46

witness said Cannon used the Spanish word for prostitute, which angered the intense Juanita.

The irate Juanita left the doorway briefly, returning with a long knife. She plunged the blade into the sternum bone of Joe Cannon, piercing his heart. He is said to have died instantly.

As all stories did in the gold camps, this one spread rapidly among the miners. The miners then assembled into a mob that seized both Juanita and her boyfriend.

As was the wont of miners in the early-day gold camps, almost instant justice was administered. A hasty court was convened, and one man in the crowd, who was a lawyer fresh from the States, was appointed to defend Juanita.

He began to deliver his arguments while perched on a barrel, but the decision of the mob of miners had already been made. Someone kicked the barrel from beneath the lawyer, sending his hat and glasses slithering away.

Then, in complete disarray, he was carried by the mob of miners a hundred yards away before being set down, receiving a few blows along the way.

Next to come to Juanita's defense was Dr. C. D. Akins, who informed the irate miners that they should show some compassion because Juanita was pregnant.

Three other town doctors were assigned to attest to the pregnancy claim. They found Juanita was not pregnant, as Dr. Akins had claimed. Dr. Akins was given twenty-four hours to leave town.

Juanita's Mexican companion was acquitted, but Juanita was found guilty and sentenced to be hanged.

According to one writer's account, printed in the Dogtown Territorial Quarterly, Juanita bravely faced her fate.

"Three thousand excited spectators were present. On the plank she stood quietly surveying the crowd. Perceiving a friend, she took off her Panama hat and gracefully flung it to him, bidding him good-by in Spanish. She took the rope in her own hand, placed it about her neck and adjusted it beneath her beautiful black hair with her own fingers. A white handkerchief was than thrown over her face, her hands were tied behind her and at each end of the plank, axe in hand, stood a man ready to cut the lashes. Another fired a pistol as a signal, and the axes fell. She dropped three feet, meeting her death with scarcely a struggle."

The news that Downieville had hanged a woman spread quickly throughout California and the world, shocking some citizens that lynch law had reached such an extreme.

Downieville's miners later engaged in something of a reform crusade. The reason was that Miss Sarah Pellet, a well-known temperance lecturer, was scheduled to speak at the next Fourth of July celebration.

When the day arrived, miners by the thousands came to hear Miss Pellet. When a speaker preceding Miss Pellet babbled on far too long to suit the anxious miners, someone fired a shot in the air to shut him up.

This incited a duel between the orator and one of the miners. The orator was killed and Miss Pellet quickly left town.

Miners then flocked to Downieville's saloons, completely forgetting their previous vows of temperance.

Chapter 6

Clara Bow

The 'It' Girl

Clara Bow will forever be the "It" girl. This was the description pinned on her when she starred in a movie with that name.

As biographers Jeanine Basinger and Alfred Knopf said in their 1999 book, *Silent Stars*, "Clara Bow lit up the screen as much as—if not more than—any other star in history."

She was idolized by a nation. William Cramer in his *Clara Bow: A Short Biography*, wrote, "Clara Bow invented the notion of sex on the silver screen. She was the finest actress who visibly flaunted her sex appeal and, in turn, became the most talked-about resident of Hollywood."

Clara became the icon for sexual freedom for women everywhere.

She was born in a Brooklyn tenement in 1905, and was unwanted from the day she was born. Clara was the daughter of a

Clara Bow

49

schizophrenic mother and a sexually abusive father.

Clara was not allowed to invite anyone to her home, where her mother often "entertained visiting firemen or *uncles*."

Eventually, she borrowed fifty cents from her father to get a cheap tintype photo made up so she could enter into a contest. She won the 1921 Fame and Fortune Contest and was able to break away from her nightmarish childhood. The contest was sponsored by Brewster Publications, which published Motion Picture, a favorite magazine of Clara's.

At the time, she was only sixteen years old, but full of both confidence and enthusiasm. She was given five different screen tests, and in each one, her emotional range of expression provoked great enthusiasm from every contest judge who saw the tests.

As part of her prize for winning, she was promised a role in a motion picture. Her role was for "Beyond the Rainbow," in which she was cast as a flirtatious debutante who stirs up trouble by passing the note, *"Consult you conscience. Your secret is common gossip."*

Unfortunately, Clara's sequence was cut from the movie. Still, she bounced back and landed a role in *"Down to the Sea in Ships."* She was paid $35 a week to play Dot Morgan, a full-of-fun and energetic young girl.

In her next films, "Enemies of Women" and "The Daring Years", Clara received no billing. It was film agent Maxine Alton who convinced B.P. Schulberg to audition Clara for a three-month contract at $50 a week.

Clara was subjected to a brutal audition for the contract, said Alton. *"Without makeup, still in a sweater and skirt, she ran the gamut of emotions. Schulberg told her to laugh. She did. Suddenly he said, 'Stop laughing, cry!' Immediately, in the snap of a finger, a flood of tears drenched her cheeks. She was an emotional machine. Schulberg turned to me, threw up his hands, and said, 'You win!'"*

Clara made 25 pictures during the next two years. Often it was because Schulberg loaned out his underpaid employees to other producers. Despite the grueling schedule, Clara was happy to be working as an actress.

Her real life escapades were scandalous in nature and she became fodder for the media. Paramount Pictures dumped her because of the reputation she garnered.

She decided to quit films after suffering a nervous breakdown during the filming of her final Paramount picture, "Kick In."

Clara married Rex Bell and the couple moved to Searchlight Nevada. Eventually, after a long rest, Clara was again called back to the bright lights of Hollywood.

She played in "Call Her Savage" (1932) and "Hoopla" (1933). Both were successful and financially rewarding. Clara decided to retire. She returned to Searchlight, Nevada, and had two sons of her own.

Hollywood scandal sheets began a wicked and unending campaign. She was characterized as a wild, sex-crazed, uncontrollable, and one-dimensional actress. This would continue until her death on September 26, 1965.

Many of her movies are now being brought out anew and preserved. In addition to her silent films, her 11 talking films are also being preserved.

Chapter 7

Mary Ballou:

Gold Rush Boardinghouse Keeper

*(Author's Note: No editor could say what Mary Bal-
lou had to say as well as her poignant letter says it,
spelling and grammar aside. No attempt was made to
correct the grammar or punctuation in this letter. The
only editing of the letter was to break it into para-
graphs to make it more readable.)*

Living conditions in the gold camps were indeed
harsh, perhaps more so for the few women in the
roughshod towns than for the men.

Mary Ballou, who ran a boarding
house during the California Gold
Rush, described her living accom-
modations in a letter to her son, Selden, in 1852.

"All the kitchen that I have is
four posts stuck down into the
ground and covered over the top
with factory cloth no floor but the
ground. this is a Boarding House
kitchen. There is a floor in the din-
ing room and my sleeping room covered with nothing
but cloth. We are working in a
Boarding House.

Mary Ballou
(California State
Library)

53

"Oct 27 this morning I awoke and it rained in torrents, well I got up and I thought of my House. I went and looket into my kitchen, the mud and water was over my Shoes I could not go into the kichen to do any work to day but keep perfectly dry in the Dining so I got along very well. Your Father put on his Boots and done the work in the kitchen. I felt badly to think that I was de(s)tine to be in such a place. I wept for a while and then I commenced singing and made up a song as I went.

"now I will try to tell you what my work is in this Board House. well, sometimes I am washing and Ironing sometimes I am making mince pie and Apple pie and squash pies. Sometimes frying mince turnovers and Donuts.

"I make biscuit and sometimes Indian jonny cake and then again I am making minute puding filled with rasons and Indian Bake puddings and then again a nice Plum Puding and then again I am Stuffing a Ham of pork that cost forty cents a pound.

"Sometimes I am making gruel for the sick, now and then cooking oisters sometimes making coffee for the French people strong enough for any man to walk on that has Faith as Peter had.

"three times a day I set my Table which is about thirty feet in length and do all the little fixings about it such as filling pepper boxes and vinegar cruits and mustard pots and Butter cups.

"sometimes I am feeding my chickens and then again I am scareing the Hogs out of my kitchen and Driving the mules out of my Dining room. you can see by the descrption of that I have given you of my kitchen that anything can walk into the kitchen and then from kitchen to the Dining room so you see the Hogs and mules can walk in any time day or night if they choose to do so.

sometimes I am up all times a night scaring the Hogs and mules out of the House. last night there a large rat came down pounce down onto our bed in the night. Sometimes I take my fan and try to fan myself but I work so hard that my Arms pain me so severely that I kneed some one to fan me so I do not find much comfort anywhere.

"I made a Bluberry puding to day for Dinner. Sometimes I am making soaps and cramberry tarts and Baking chicken that cost four Dollars a head and cooking Eggs at three Dollars a Dozen. Sometimes boiling cabbage and Turnips and frying fritters and Broiling stake and cooking codfish and potatoes. I often cook nice Salmon trout that weigh from ten to twenty pounds apiece.

"sometimes I am taking care of Babies and nursing at the rate of Fifty Dollars a week but I would not advise any Lady to come out her and suffer the toil and fatigue that I have suffered for the sake of a little gold neither do I advise any one to come.

"Clarks Simmon wife says if she was safe in the States she would not care if she had not one cent. She came in here last night and said, 'Oh dear I am so homesick that I must die,' and then again my other associate came in with tears in her yes and said that she had cried all day.

"she said if she had as good a home as I had got she would not stay twenty minutes in California. I told

55

her that she could not pick up her duds in that time. she said she would not stop for duds nor anything else but my own heart was two sad to cheer them much.

(Editor's note: The reference to "in the States" indicated how far from home the gold miners felt because California was not a state at this time)

"now I will tell you a little more about my cooking. Sometimes I am cooking rabbits and Birds that are called quails here and I cook squrrels. occasionly I run in and have a chat with Jane and Mrs. Durphy and I often have a hearty cry. no one but my maker knows my feelings. and then I run into my little cellar which is about four feet square as I have no other place to run that is cool.

"October 21 well I have been to church to hear a Methodist sermon. his text was let us lay aside every weight and the sin that doth so easely beset us. I was the only Lady that was present and about forty gentlemen. So you see that I go to church when I can.

"November 2 well it has been Lexion here to day. I have heard of struggling and tite pulling but never saw such aday as I have witnessed to day the Ballot Box was so near to me that I could hear every word that was spoken.

"the wind blows very hard here tto day. I have three lights Burning and the wind blows so hard that it almost puts my lights out while I am trying to write. If you could but step in and see the inconvenience that I have for writing you would not wonder that I cannot write any better you would wonder that I could write at all.

"notwithstanding all the dificuty in writing I improve every leishure moment. it is quite cool here my fingers are so cold that I can hardly hold my pen.

"well it is ten o'clock at night while I am writing. the people have been Declareing the votes. I hear them say Hura for the Whigs and sing whigs songs. now I hear them say that Morman Island has gone whig and now another time a cheering, now I hear them say Beals Bar has gone whig now another time of cheering. well it is getting late and I must retire soon there is so much noise I do not expect to sleep much to night. there has been a little fighting here to day and one challenge given but the chalenge given but the chalenge given was not accepted they got together and setted their trouble.

"I will tell you a little of my bad feelings, on the 9 of September there was a little fight took place in the store. I saw them strike each other though the window in the store. One went and got a pistol and started towards the other man.

"I never go into the store but your mothers tender heart could not stand that so I ran into the store and Beged and plead with him not to kill him for eight or ten minutes not to take his Life for the sake of his wife and three little children to spare his life and then I ran through the Dining room into my sleeping room and Buried my Face in my bed so as not to hear the sound of the pistol and wept Biterly.

"Oh I thought if I had wings how quick I would fly to the States. that night at the supper table he told the Boarders if it had not been for what that Lady said to him Scheles would have been a dead man. after he got

57

his pashion over he said that he was glad that he did not kill him so you see that your mother has saved one Human beings Life, you see that I am trying to relieve all the suffering and trying to do all the good that I can.

"there I hear the Hogs in my kichen turning the Pots and kettles upside down so I must drop my pen and run and drive them out. so you see this is the way that I have to write—jump up every five minutes for something and then again I washed out about a Dollars worth of gold dust the fourth of July in the cradle so you see that I am doing a little mining in this gold region but I think it harder to rock the cradle to wash out gold than it is to rock the cradle for Babies in the states.

"October 11 I washed in the forenoon and made a Democrat Flag in the afternoon sewed twenty yards of splendid worsted fringe around it and I made whig flag. I had twelve Dollars for making them so you see that I am making Flags with all rest of the various kinds of work that I am doing and then again I am scouring candlesticks and washing floor and making soft soap. The people tell me that it is the first Soft Soap they knew made in California.

"Sometimes I am making mattresses and sheets. I have no windows in my room. all the light that I have shines through a canvas that covers the House and my eyes are so dim that I can hardly see to make a mark so I think you will excuse me for not writing any better. I have three Lights burning now but I am so tired and Blind that I can scarcely see and her I am among the French and Duch and Scoth and Jews and Italions and Sweeds and Chineese and Indians and all manner of tongus and nations but I am treated with due respect by them all.

"I imagine you will say what a long yarn this is from California. if you can read it at all I must close soon for I am so tired and almost sick. Oh my Dear Selden I am so Home sick I will say to you once more to see that Augustus has every thing he kneeds to make him comfortable and by all means have him Dressed warm this cold winter. I worry a great deal about my Dear children. it seems as though my heart would break when I realize how far I am from my Dear Loved ones this from your affectionate mother."

Mary B. Ballou

Chapter 8

Amelia Earhart

She Conquered Men's Worlds

From the time Amelia Earhart crawled into the open-cockpit plane at Daugherty Field in Long Beach to fly over Los Angeles, she knew then she would enter an area previously reserved for men.

She had not been impressed, however, when saw her first airplane at the Iowa State fair at ten years of age. "It was a thing of rusty wire and wood and not at all interesting," she later recalled.

It wasn't 1920 that her aviation interest was sparked. She attended an "aerial meet" with her father at Daugherty Field in Long Beach.

The following day, she was given a helmet and goggles, and she boarded the

Amelia Earhart during flight stopover.

open-cockpit biplane for a ten-minute flight over Los Angeles.

Amelia was hooked. "As soon as we left the ground I knew I had to fly!" And fly she did, undoubtedly inspiring women across the nation to take up flying. Amelia learned of Anita

Amelia Earhart

"Neta" Snook, a female pilot who was an instructor at Kinner Field near Long Beach, and she began taking flying lessons from her. Her early flying abilities came into question, not only by Neta Snook, but many of her contemporaries as well. Amelia was a bit reckless and had several accidents, but some of these were attributed to the unreliability of the early airplanes.

Amelia began participating in a number of record-breaking attempts. She set a women's altitude record of 14,000 feet. This was broken a few weeks later by Ruth Nichols.

Her fame as a flyer continued to spread. One day, she received a phone call from Captain H.H. Railey, asking her, "...how would you like to be the first woman to fly across the Atlantic?"

No woman had so far flown across the Atlantic. Railey, taken with the strong resemblance Amelia had with Charles Lindbergh, called her "Lady Lindy."

Amelia had no experience with multi-engine aircraft or instrument flying. Wilmer Stultz and Louis Gordon would pilot the tri-motor Fokker named the "Friendship". Amelia was given the title of "commander" of the flight.

"I was a passenger on the journey...just a passenger," Amelia said later. "Everything that was done to bring us across was done by Wilmer Stultz and Slim Gordon. Any praise I can give them they ought to have—I do not believe that women lack the stamina to do a solo trip across the Atlantic, but it would be a matter of learning the arts of flying by instruments only, an art which few men pilots know perfectly now."

Amelia was distressed that reporters ignored the pilots of the flight, putting all their attention on her, when she was only a passenger.

Aviation was a new concept in the 1920s. Amelia was appointed Assistant to the General Traffic Manager at Transcontinental air Transport (later known as TWA) with a special responsibility of attracting women passengers.

In 1929, Amelia organized a cross-country air race for women pilots. The race would be from Los Angeles to the Cleveland Women's Air Derby. Will Rogers labeled the event as "The Powder Puff Derby," a name that stuck!

Amelia later formed the "Ninety-Nines", a women pilot's organization. Charter membership included ninety-nine applicants.

By 1932, no other person had successfully flown solo across the Atlantic since Lindbergh's historic flight. Amelia wanted to be the next one to do so.

She veered somewhat off-course near the end of her flight, and landed in an open field near Londonderry in Northern Ireland. She climbed from her plane, and asked an approaching man, "Where am I?"

He replied, "In Gallegher's pasture...have you come far?"

"From America," she said.

She had broken several records on the flight. She was the first woman to fly the Atlantic solo and the only person to fly it twice. She had made the longest non-stop distance flown by a woman, and she had set a record for crossing in the shortest time.

Always seeking new goals, Amelia then decided to try flying a trans-Pacific flight from Hawaii to California...and then on to Washington, D.C. Ten pilots had lost their lives attempting this flight.

When she arrived in Oakland, California, to a cheering crowd of thousands, President Roosevelt sent his congratulations. "You have scored again and showed that aviation is a science which cannot be limited to men only," the President wrote."

She soon began planning her next venture. This would be a trip around the world, traveling the longest possible route by circumnavigating the earth at its equator.

Her navigator on the trip would be Frederick Noonan who had been a navigator on the Pan American Pacific Clipper. When they took off from Luke Field, near Pearl Harbor, Amelia over-compensated for a dropped wing and the plane went out of control. The wrecked Electra was shipped back to California and

Amelia continued with her plans for another attempt at flying around the world.

In this attempt, she decided to reverse her course because of weather conditions in the Caribbean and in Africa.

"I have a feeling that there is just about one more good flight left in my system and I hope this I it. Anyway, when I have finished this job, I mean to give up long-distance 'stunt' flying," she told reporters.

Earhart and Noonan planned this time to fly from Miami, Florida, go around the world, and land in California. Their first destination was San Juan Puerto Rico. From there, they would skirt the northeast edge of South America and then fly on to Africa and the Red Sea.

When Amelia and Noonan reached Lae, in New Guinea, they had flown 22,000 miles. They still had 7,000 to go, all over the Pacific Ocean. Amelia cabled her last commissioned article to the Herald Tribune. Photos of Amelia during her time in Lae, showed her very tired and perhaps ill.

Amelia and her navigator left Lae at precisely 00:00 hours Greenwich Mean Time (GMT) on July 2, 1937. Their plane, the Electra, was believed loaded with 1,000 gallons of fuel, enough for 20 to 21 hours of flying.

At 08:00 GMT, she made her last radio contact with Lae. She reported she was on course for Howland Island and flying at 12,000 feet.

At 19:30 GMT, the following transmission was received from Amelia by the Coast Guard Cutter Itasca, which was standing off Howland Island.

"KHAQQ calling Itasca. We must be on you but cannot see you...gas is running low..."

At 20:14 GMT, the Itasca received the last voice transmission from Amelia, giving positioning data. The Coast Guard determined that Amelia must have ditched at sea.

Extensive search efforts failed to find any parts of the craft, even though it was believed the plane's empty gas tanks would have kept it afloat for a period of time.

Many rumors have floated about unconfirmed sightings of Amelia's craft. Among them:

- Amelia was on a spy mission authorized by President Roosevelt and was captured.
- She purposely dove her plane into the Pacific.
- She was captured by the Japanese and forced to broadcast to American GI's as "Tokyo Rose" during World War II.
- She lived for years on an island in the South Pacific with a native fisherman.

While the search goes on, including a web site by The International Group for Historic Aircraft Recovery (TIGHAR), it may never be learned how or where Amelia finally crashed. The trail grows dim.

Chapter 9

Clara Shortridge Foltz

California's First Woman Lawyer

Clara Shortridge Foltz grew angry as she listened to the district attorney present his closing argument to the San Francisco jury. He concluded by attempting to discredit her as an attorney for the defendant.

"She is a WOMAN! She can't be expected to reason. God Almighty decreed her limitations...this young woman will lead you by her sympathetic presentation of this case to violate your oaths and let a guilty man go free!"

It wasn't the first time she had been accused of being weak and unqualified being awarded her law degree.

Clara Foltz

But she rose to the task before her and demolished the legal and ad hominem arguments of the prosecutor.

67

She won her case.

The year was 1870. Clara Foltz was California's first woman attorney and she faced opposition from both sexes when she applied for entrance to the state bar. But because of her perseverance she opened the profession to future generations of California women.

Clara married Iowa farmer Jeremiah Foltz at a young age. She was only fifteen when the couple eloped in 1865. Three years later, Jeremiah moved his wife and three children to Portland, Oregon.

There, Clara started a dressmaking business to help make ends meet. She had barely started making a profit when the sheriff arrived to confiscate her sewing machine to pay for her husband's debts.

She was angered that no lawyer would represent her in the case. This led to her vow to one day learn the law for herself and fight for the rights of women.

Clara and Jeremiah then moved to San Jose, California. At this time, the couple had four children and Clara was pregnant with a fifth. San Jose was home to a strong women's suffrage movement and Clara threw herself into the fight with all her heart.

Her husband abandoned her and the children two years later. She continued her fight for the cause of women. She began earning money as a public speaker in support of women's rights.

"Genius, talent, and hard labor know no sex," Clara shouted to her audiences. At the same time, she began studying for the California bar.

She faced a monumental obstacle, however. California law had strict provisions on who could join the bar. An applicant had to be 21 years of age, white, of good moral character, in possession of learning and ability, and most forbiddingly, must be MALE.

Clara engaged the help of Laura deForce Gordon, a strong activist in the suffrage movement. Together, they drew up the "Women's Lawyer Bill." The bill simply changed the word 'male' to 'person'.

When the bill came up for a vote before the California Legislature in 1878, Clara made the trip to Sacramento in the caboose of a cattle train, eating only hard biscuits and boiled eggs she had stuffed in her pockets.

Clara's Women's Lawyer Bill met with a wall of opposition. In her autobiography, she wrote:

> "The bill met with a storm of opposition such as had never been witnessed upon the floor of a California Senate. Narrow-gauge statesmen grew as red as turkey gobblers mouthing their ignorance against the bill, and staid old grangers who had never seen the inside of a courthouse seemed to have been given the gift of tongues and they delivered themselves of maiden speeches pregnant with eloquent nonsense."

Yet, Senate Bill 66 passed the Senate by a vote of 22-11 and moved its way through the Assembly a few days later.

Her battle wasn't over. The legislature was in the last day of its session, and as midnight approached, the governor had not yet signed the Women's Lawyer Bill.

When a politician emerged from the governor's office declaring the bill as dead, Clara stormed into the governor's office to confront him herself. The governor, she wrote, sat at a large table in the center of the room, surrounded by legislators.

69

Foltz came through the crowd and politely asked him to sign Senate Bill 66. "The governor continued to lift up bill after bill in that huge stack of discarded ones and finally, aided by a clerk, the bill was fished out and laid all but dead before him."

Governor William Irwin signed the bill just before the clock struck twelve.

Later in the same year, Clara passed a three-hour oral exam to become California's first licensed female attorney.

She didn't let her success at gaining entry to the bar stop her efforts to gain legal reform and women's rights.

Foltz' fought hard to become a lawyer. The thorny battle to overcome male prejudice was reported in a treatise in the Hastings Law Journal. Mortimer D. Schwartz, Susan L. Brandt, and Patience Milrod wrote the heavily documented paper.

A fighter by nature, Foltz boasted, "I am descended from the heroic stock of Daniel Boone and never shrank from contest nor knew a fear. I inherit no drop of craven blood."

After winning her first couple of cases in court, Clara decided to attend Hastings College for more traditional legal schooling. The college denied her admission.

Clara sued, and tried the case herself and won. She then paid the ten-dollar tuition fee, but when she arrived for her first class, the school janitor met her at the door.

"Miss, this is a law school. I'm ordered not to let you come in here," he told her. She had to obtain a note from Judge Hastings directing the janitor to let her enter, although the judge himself warned it might only be temporary, depending upon a decision by the school's board of directors.

Resistance to women at the school was not confined to administrators. She recalled in her autobiography:

"The first day I had a bad cold and was forced to cough. To my astonishment every young man in the class was seized with a violent fit of coughing. You would have thought the whooping cough was a raging epidemic among the little fellows. If I turned over a leaf in my notebook, every student in the class did likewise. If I moved my chair—hitch went every chair in the room. I don't know what ever became of the members of that class. They must have been an inferior lot, for certain it is, I have never seen nor heard tell of one of them from that day to this."

Her tenure in class was short lived. Two days later Hastings College's board of directors denied her application for admission.

Foltz decided to fight this decision, too. She applied for a writ of mandamus to the Fourth District Court in San Francisco to compel Hastings' board of directors to admit women.

She won her case, but not before the directors appealed the decision of Judge R.F. Morrison, hoping that Clara would gave up her cause as her determination wore thin and her money ran out.

While waiting for the Supreme Court to hear the case, Clara studied for and passed the exam for admission to the state Supreme Court bar.

She represented herself before the court where she faced substantially the same arguments advanced by the directors in the district court. She won her case, and later said the case was "the greatest in my more than half century before the bar."

Finally, she was able to take her place among the law students at Hastings. She stayed there for two years, but her increasing practice made attendance difficult.

Her undaunted efforts were gaining her a growing list of clients. She set up law offices in cities such as San Diego, Denver and New York. She encountered male prejudice everywhere she went.

Once, an opposing attorney referred to her as a "lady lawyer." Clara glibly answered that she could not return the compliment for she "had never heard anybody call him any kind of lawyer at all."

Clara Foltz next spearheaded a movement to improve prison conditions and state parole systems. She urged the separation of juvenile and adult prisoners. She then led a movement that established public defender systems, which provided legal representation for those too poor to pay.

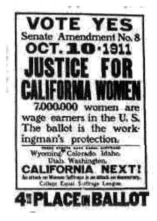

Continuing her fight for women's rights, Clara is credited with drafting California's suffrage law, which passed in 1911.

She ran for governor of California in 1930 at the age of eighty-one. She received 3,570 votes in the Republican primary.

Clara held no illusions about her chances. She wrote a friend during the campaign: "I have no illusions as to the outcome of this last courageous effort of mine—I simply must go right on demonstrating our great cause."

Chapter 10

Women Printers

They led way into men's domain

Women worked from morn to dusk and even longer in the gold camps, but they would have a hard time finding a job in any kind of business.

In a deftly written article appearing in the Dogtown Territorial Quarterly in 1997, Dr. Robert J. Chandler points out the difficulties women had entering the labor force. Dr. Chandler is a senior researcher for Historical Services, Wells Fargo Bank, San Francisco.

He cited Hermoine Day, editor of the San Francisco monthly Hesperian, in 1858. "When we mention school teaching, and keeping boarders, we have covered the entire ground upon which women may labor for her daily bread, " wrote Miss Day.

Jacqueline Barnhart cited the situation in her book, *"The Fair But Frail"* (1986). Women considered to be of "lower class" could only become laundresses and domestic servants, while those slightly higher could go into sewing, cooking, and clerking—all at poor wages.

It is interesting to note, however, that one woman who came to California with her husband during the gold rush, was more adept at making money than her husband. By taking in the laundry of miners, she made more during a month than her husband did panning for gold.

According to Dr. Chandler's research, in the decade of the 1860s, San Francisco's population doubled and women seized the opportunity to provide shelter.

"In 1869," said Chandler, "women ran 61 percent of the boarding and lodging houses."

One might imagine the angst of women in 1863 when John Swett, superintendent of public instruction, formed the professional California Education Society. Its constitution restricted membership to "male members only."

It was close to ten years before women could become members, even though their teaching numbers soon exceeded the number of men. Men also were paid higher wages for teaching. In 1864, male teachers in the state averaged $74 monthly, while their female counterparts received only $55.

In 1870, the legislature required San Francisco schools to pay equally "for similar services in the same grades," and in 1874, women lobbied successfully to have this rule extended throughout the state.

Only nine counties paid somewhat equal pay. San Francisco continued to pay men almost two times as much as it paid the women doing the same work.

Sophia E. Walker, who wrote under the pen name of "Lisle Lester", took up the challenge to get women into the typographical union. She employed women as printers on her San Francisco *Pacific Monthly*".

The California Historical Society says California was not the first place where women were involved in printing and publishing. Women had been part of the printing trades in Europe since the Renaissance.

A woman's typographical union was formed in France with a journal entitled *La Compositrice.* The first major woman's journal edited by a woman, *Godey's Lady's Book,* was published in Philadelphia from 1830-1858.

These 19th Century women faced union resistance, prejudice against women working in a male work force, and general problems encountered in owning their own businesses.

Women who were widows or daughters of printers often learned typesetting out of necessity, said the California Historical Society.

During the 19th century, women writers also moved into positions as editors of newspapers or small journals.

Slow as it was to act, California's legislature did try to address some of the women's issues. On April 12, 1852, the legislature attempted to place married women on an economic equality with their single sisters, wrote historian Chandler.

The lawmakers declared that married women could transact business in their own "Name as Sole Trader," and that the property, revenue, moneys, and debts, and credits so invested, shall belong exclusively to said married woman."

Mary A. Fledge, wife of Henry Fledge, promptly inserted a notice in the Petaluma *Journal* that she "would carry on business in my own name, as sole trader," and that the business would be "farming and stock raising, also the raising of poultry, in the county of Sonoma."

According to historian Chandler, in the winter of 1866-1867, the *Alta California* proclaimed, "work and fair play must be provided for women." The newspaper wanted to open new employments, now filled exclusively by men, to women.

Another newspaper, the DeYoung brothers' *Dramatic Chronicle* went a step further. It denounced a society that would train women only to be "featherbrained dolls with shallow hearts and unfurnished minds."

The paper urged that women be allowed to do honorable work that she can do well, be it mechanical or professional, and be paid as much as men.

The gold rush period was especially harsh on society women who were down on their luck. About the only trade in which they could engage was keeping boarders or prostitution, which was so repugnant to most that it wasn't a consideration.

The 1860 San Francisco directory listed one hundred forty boarding houses and forty lodging houses, which did not provide food. Women kept forty-nine percent of them.

A survey made in 1872 of women mostly employed in book binding and clothing manufacturing, found that women averaged $9 a week, a little more than common day laborers. Saleswomen made from $6 to $8, while factory workers made $3 to $10.

In 1865, a person who simply signed herself as "Lady Subscriber", advocated in the San Francisco *Alta California* that the "most prominent men and women" of the city form a society to provide jobs such as bookkeeping, store sales, and cigar and harness making." The person, who dubbed herself as "Lady Subscriber", said "Women should learn to depend upon themselves alone."

Chapter 11

Olive Mann Isbell

She wrote lessons on the dirt floor

Inside Mission Santa Clara de Asis, the future looked grim for the 130 Americans. The gates of the crumbling Mission were barricaded to keep out the Spanish soldiers of Don Francisco Sanchez, who appeared on the verge of attacking the newly arrived emigrants.

There was a climate of fear inside the mission, especially among the children. Olive Mann Isbell, the niece of Horace Mann and a former teacher herself, could see the children needed both attention and a haven. She set the children and any others who would volunteer to clean an old 15-square-foot adobe stable. A rickety table and a few benches were thrown together from scraps of wood left in the compound.

Olive Mann Isbell

"Before you get started, you'll have to learn how to use this," said a man who handed her a long rifle. When classes began, she kept the weapon handy.

Mrs. Mann lacked even pencils and paper. She wrote lessons on the dirt floor with a long pointed stick. From each spent fire she saved the charcoal and wrote the youngsters' A-B-Cs on the palms of their hands. Olive Mann Isbell soon became Aunt Olive to the children, who tried to imitate her courage.

Thus began the first school in California taught by an American.

Many of the emigrants in the compound were sick, including Olive's husband, Dr. Chauncy Isbell, a medical graduate of Western Reserve College. The Isbells came west with $2000 in reserve funds and a well-fitted wagon.

As they crossed the Sierra Nevada, John Fremont met them at a pass near Bear River and escorted them to Sutter's Fort and then on to the Mission.

Dr. Isbell was drafted to join Fremont and his men. However, upon crossing the Salinas River, he was stricken with typhoid pneumonia, the so-called 'emigrant fever' and returned to the Mission.

Olive's knowledge of drugs and nursing served her well as she tended to her ill husband and others suffering sickness. While her patients slept, Olive made bullets to hold off their attackers.

When Dr. Isbell became well enough to travel, he and his wife moved to Monterey. When they arrived, they learned the Mexican War had ended and California was about to become a member of the United States.

On her very first night in Monterey, Thomas O. Larkin, United States Consul, who had heard of her previous school at the Mission, called on Olive. Larkin wanted her to set up a similar school in Monterey.

Dr. Isbell began a medical practice, and Olive opened a school with about two dozen students. This number soon grew to about fifty, with each student paying six dollars for a term of three months.

Unlike the conditions in the Mission, Olive opened a classroom with a few books, and with some pencils and paper. The school was located above the jail. Only two of her students knew how to speak English. A tutor helped Mrs. Isbell, who spoke no Spanish.

The Isbells soon moved to French Camp, a community near Tuleberg, where Stockton now sits. They had barely settled when gold was discovered at Sutter's Mill. Dr. Isbell and others organized the Stockton Mining Company and set out for the gold fields.

Once when it was so muddy the horses could not travel on the road, Dr. Isbell showed up with a young boy to help him carry eighty pounds of gold in sacks.

While Dr. Isbell was away mining, the twenty-four-year-old Olive was left to care for the horses, chickens, milk cows and 600 head of cattle. Her only help was a nine-year-old boy.

She discovered the Indians liked the type of clothing she wore. She made an outfit every day, which she traded for two ounces of gold. She soon found herself cooking meals for travelers, for which she charged a modest sum. She received $500 in gold when she sent a wagon to Stockton filled with two demijohns of milk, two of cream, some eggs, four-dozen chickens, and a few pounds of butter.

By 1850, the Isbells had become wealthy. The couple had no children. Dr. Isbell wanted to travel and convinced his reluctant wife to sell their French Camp holdings.

Eventually, they returned to California and settled in Santa Paula. Olive died there on March 25, 1899.

Chapter 12

Helen Hunt Jackson

Her book, 'Ramona', is a classic

Helen Hunt Jackson literally wrote her way into California History. She was headstrong and determined. It was evident to those who knew her that once she set her mind to something, she would find a way.

Helen Hunt Jackson

She married Edward Bissell Hunt, a West Point man. She bore him two sons, the first of which died before his first birthday.

In October 1863, Major Hunt died from escaping gas while testing an underwater naval vessel. Her second son Rennie died of diphtheria at age ten.

Facing a bout of depression, Helen turned to writing, and some of her early poems appeared in such prominent New York publications as Hearth and Home, New York Evening Post, Nation, and Atlantic Monthly.

When her writing failed to pull her out of her depression, Helen sought help from the hot mineral waters in Colorado. Staying at the same hotel was William Sharpless Jackson, a wealthy banker and treasurer of the Denver and Rio Grande Railroad. They became close and married in 1875.

Always considered a scholar, Helen began making daily visits to nearby Indian camps, where Indian children reminded her of her two dead sons.

Helen's interest in Indian Affairs was intensified when she met members of the Indian Commission at a reception in Boston. It was the Ponca Chief, Standing Bear, that convinced Helen of the tragic plight of his people.

Chief Standing Bear described the forcible removal of Ponca Indians from their Nebraska reservation. Helen vowed to help raise funds to improve the condition of the Indians

Ignoring a plea from her husband Will to come home and give up her fight for the Indians, Helen instead went to New York City and spent three months digging up facts at the Astor Library about the U.S. Government's mistreatment of Indians.

This led to her writing "A Century of Dishonor," which she considered her most important book. The book did arouse voters, senators and congressmen.

President Chester Arthur asked that Helen be appointed a special commissioner for the Bureau of Indian Affairs. She accepted the assignment to report on the Indian conditions in southern California.

She met Don Antonio Coronel, former mayor of Los Angeles (1853-54), who was an authority on early Californio life. She learned that the Indians in southern California were no better off than Indians elsewhere.

In discussing secularization in 1833, Coronel told Jackson, "When Americans assumed control, they ignored the Indian claims to lands, leading to their mass dispossessions."

Don Coronel's accounts galvanized Jackson to action. Her work on behalf of the dispossessed Indians came to the attention of U.S. Commissioner of Indian Affairs, Hiram Price. He recommended Jackson be appointed as Interior Department agent to visit the Mission Indians in California.

Helen was sure that whatever report she wrote would be thrown aside and dismissed, just as her book, "A Century of Dishonor" had been. Nevertheless, she kept prodigious notes, recording every detail of her journey and the conditions of the missions and the needs of the Indians.

Jackson heard of the senseless killing of a Cahuilla Indian. The story concerned Juan Diego, who had a wife and a baby. Diego went off to find work and he came home riding a strange horse. A white man named Temple, who was the owner of the horse, awakened Juan from sleep. Temple leveled his gun and shot the Indian dead."

In San Jacinto, Jackson looked up the records of the case, which would become the focus of her novel, "Ramona."

In a letter to Atlantic Monthly's editor, Helen wrote: "I have never before felt that I could write an Indian story. I had not the background that I now have, and sooner or later, I shall write the story. If I could write a story that would do for the Indian a thousandth part of what Uncle Toms Cabin did for the Negro, I would be thankful the rest of my life."

Jackson criss-crossed Southern California, traveling with Indian agent Abbot Kinney. Together, they documented the appalling conditions of the Indians.

At one point, she hired a law firm to protect the rights of a family of Soboba Indians facing dispossession of their land at the foot of the San Jacinto Mountains.

As she had predicted, Washington officials largely ignored her report. In the 56-page report, Helen asked for a massive government relief effort, ranging from the purchase of new lands for reservations to the establishment of more Indian schools. A bill embodying many of her recommendations passed the Senate but died in the House.

It was then that Jackson decided to write a novel that would depict the Indian conditions. She was particularly drawn to the fate of her Indian friends in the Temecula area of Riverside County.

She recalled, in writing Ramona, *"As soon as I began, it seemed impossible to write fast enough...I wrote faster than I would write a letter...two thousand to three thousand words in a morning, and I cannot help it."*

From the first day of the book's issue sales were staggering. "I do not dare think I have written a second Uncle Toms Cabin," she told a friend, "but I do think I have written a story which will be a good stroke for the Indian cause."

The public took Ramona to heart and brought pressure upon the government to act on some of Jackson's recommendations.

In California, Juan Diego's killer left the state to avoid ridicule, even though the killing had been considered self-defense. In her book, however, the killing of Ramona's Allessandro was murder.

Chapter 13

Lillie Coit

'She wanted to be one of the boys"

At the age of eight, Lillie Hitchcock was trapped when fire raged through a building she and two other youngsters were exploring.

As she stood in the midst of a ring of flames, above her, John Boynton, hacked a hole through the roof. He was a substitute on San Francisco's Knickerbocker Number Five fire company.

Boynton lowered himself on a rope, and carried Lillie on his back while clambering hand-over-hand

back up the rope to safety. The other youngsters perished in the fire.

From then on, Lillie's affection for Knickerbocker No. 5 continued to grow.

At age fifteen, the fire company had a short staff on the ropes as it raced to a fire on Telegraph Hill. Because of the shortage of manpower, the engine was falling behind. It would be humiliating to the firemen if Manhattan No. 2 or Howard No. 3 beat Knicker-

Lillie Coit

91

bocker to the fire. It was then that Lillie, on her way home from school, took action.

Lillie tossed her books to the sidewalk and dashed to a vacant place on the rope. At the same time, Lillie cried out to the bystanders, "Come on, you men! Everybody pull and we'll beat 'em!"

And the bystanders did come and pull and Knickerbocker No. 5 hurled up the slope and put "first water" on the fire.

From that day on, Lillie caught the spirit of the Volunteer Firemen, and they in turn responded. There was never a gala parade in which Lillie was not seen atop Knickerbocker No. 5. She was, literally, the patroness of all the firemen of her city.

Lillie was always something of a "tomboy". As a child, she romped in short frocks and was fascinated by the red shirt and warlike helmets worn by firemen. She gloried in the excitement of a big blaze.

While still in her teens, Lillie rushed to the scene of every fire when she heard the fire bell toll its alarms. She came to be regarded as a mascot by the firemen.

On October 3, 1863, Lillie was elected an honorary member of the Knickerbocker Company, and always regarded that honor as the proudest of her life. She wore the numeral and the gold badge the firemen had presented her with all her costumes.

Lillie would leave whatever she was doing to attend a fire. Once she left a wedding party in which she was a bridesmaid.

Coit Tower

The Hitchcocks were considered valued members of San Francisco Society, and her parents, especially her mother, agonized over the actions of Lillie.

When Lillie's father, Dr. Charles Hitchcock heard about Lillie driving a team of horses at their Calistoga summer home, he didn't try to stop her. Instead, he hired Colonel Clark Foss, a noted stagecoach driver, to give her lessons.

According to one account, Lillie would often drive groups of her suitors, usually at breakneck speed to the White Sulphur Springs Hotel. Then, often as not, she beat the young men at poker while smoking cigars and helped to polish off a bottle of bourbon.

Howard Coit first saw Lillie when she was riding Knickerbocker No. 5 back from a fire. "I was surprised,"
he said later, "that she was incandescent rather than beautiful."

When Lillie sighted Coit, it was said to be love at first sight. They eloped in 1869, angering Lillie's mother who felt the young stockbroker was not good enough for her daughter.

Coit died in 1885, but he and Lillie had already been separated for five years. Their marriage had been fraught with suspicion and jealousy.

In 1904, it is reported that an assassin bent on killing her broke into her room while she was entertaining a Major McClurg. The major boldly defended her and subdued the assassin, but McClurg later died. The assassin, ruled insane by the courts, was assigned to a padded cell.

Lillie was so shaken by the event that she moved to Paris, where she lived for 20 years. It was not until the assassin died that Lillie returned to her beloved San Francisco.

When Lillie Coit died in San Francisco July 22, 1929, at the age of 86, she left one-third of her fortune to the city "to be expended in an appropriate manner for the purpose of adding to the beauty of the city which I have always loved."

The executors of her will, several years after her death, decided to erect a memorial tower in her honor and also as a memorial tribute to San Francisco's firemen.

This novel 180-foot cylindrical tower, shaped like a fire-nozzle, stands atop Telegraph Hill. A family mausoleum holds the remains of Lillie (she was cremated). Beside the niche where her ashes are stored is a khaki fire jacket, a coiled fire hose, and a brass fire hose nozzle.

Chapter 14

Charley Parkhurst

A true hero of the west

Charley Darkey Parkhurst was one of the celebrated stagecoach whips in the west. Charley's story has been told over and over, but it never fails to draw excitement with each telling.

Not everyone could manage a stagecoach. The stagecoach driver was held in higher esteem when on the summit of the Sierra than was the millionaire statesman who might be riding beside him.

While most stage drivers were sober, at least while on duty, nearly all were fond of an occasional "eye opener". A good driver was the captain of his craft. He was feared by his timid passengers, awed by stable boys, and was the trusty agent of his employer.

The seat next to the driver, weather permitting, was the preferred seat of the men passengers. But this was one seat that was reserved, and it was not gotten by simply being the first to hop on the left front wheel rim and climbing into the box.

If the driver didn't want the person who took the seat there, he would firmly order him down, and then enjoy the passenger's discomfiture for the next ten miles.

To sit in the driver's seat, one proceeded very much in the manner of securing an appointment to a high office. It sometimes required going to the source of authority—above the driver himself—to the super-intendent and even to the president of the company.

Charlie Parkhurst was one of the more skillful stagecoach drivers, not only in California, but throughout the west. He was variously called "One-eyed" or "Cockeyed" Charlie.

He got the nickname while in Redwood City, California. Charley was shoeing his lead horse Pete when the horse kicked him in the face. Charley lost an eye in the episode and thereafter wore a patch.

Charlotte Parkhurst was born in Lebanon, New Hampshire in 1812. Some accounts say he was abandoned by his parents and placed in an orphanage from which he escaped.

Charley found work in a stable owned by Ebenezer Balch in Worchester, Massachusetts. The owner was unaware that Charley was a runaway and put him to work cleaning stalls, washing carriages and scrubbing floors.

He always displayed a keen interest in learning more about horses. He carefully watched the stage drivers who drove their Concord stagecoaches into Worcester. His boss, Ebe Balch was impressed with the promise of his young protégé and taught Charley the art of driving in hand, then four-in-hand, and finally six-in-hand horse teams.

Charley soon became known as the best coachman on the eastern seaboard. Customers often hired a coach only on condition that Charley be the driver.

Once, while in Georgia, Charley drove for Jim Birch, who was getting ready to go west and operate the California Stage Line. Charley tagged along, saying, "I aim to be the best damn driver in California."

One writer, Major A.N. Judd, claimed he had traced Charley's history back to the Indian days and the overland stage line, headquartered in Council Bluffs, Iowa. The stage line was run by old Ben Holiday. There were about 50 applicants for the position open on the stage line.

"Ever driven stage? How long? How near could you drive to the edge of a bluff with a sheer drop of a thousand feet with perfect safety to your self, your team and passengers?" These were the questions fired at the applicants by Holiday.

Charley listened to the stream of applicants answering the questions. Many answered they would drive nearer and nearer until they got to the edge. Finally, one blurted he was willing to take a chance with half the tire over the edge on one wheel.

It was coming Charley's turn and he was feeling uneasy. Taking a chew of tobacco, Charley headed for the door, looked back over his shoulder, and said, "I wouldn't do at all for you, Mr. Holiday. I'd stay as far away from the edge of that cliff as the hubs would let me."

"You are just the man I want!" said Holiday.

For three years, Charley held that job and then moved to California, first driving on the Pacheco Pass run and then for the Danforth Porter lines that connected with the Santa Cruz stage line.

Carpinteria was always a welcome rest spot for passengers on Charlie Parkhurst's run. For one thing, Shepard's Inn, run by a former Iowa farmer, James Erwin Shepard had wonderful food, good beds, and pleasant hospitality.

In the shantytown of Los Angeles, there was little to attract travelers, although they could purchase ice cream and hot tamales there.

Twice Charlie was held up. The first time, he was forced to throw down his strongbox because he was unarmed. The second time, he was prepared.

When a second road agent ordered the stage to stop and commanded Charlie to throw down the strongbox, Parkhurst leveled a shotgun blast into the chest of the outlaw. He whipped his horses into a full gallop, and left the bandit in the road.

One-eyed Charlie was known as one of the toughest, roughest, and most daring of stagecoach drivers. Like most drivers, he was proud of his skill in the extremely difficult job as "whip".

Whips received high salaries for the times, sometimes as much as $125 a month, plus room and board.

"How in the world can you see your way through this dust?" one passenger asked Charlie.

"Smell it," Charlie replied. "Fact is, I've traveled over these mountains so often I can tell where the road is by the sound of the wheels. When they rattle, I'm on hard ground; when they don't rattle I gen'r'lly look over the side to see where she's agoing."

When the railroads came west, they essentially put Charley out of business.

Charley's dark secret was revealed during the 1860s, while he working for Andy Jackson Clark. Charley reportedly came home drunk. Mrs. Clark asked her seventeen-year-old son to put Charley to bed.

According to Ms. Helen T. Tarr, Clark's granddaughter, the boy returned in a dither, exclaiming, "Maw, Charley ain't no man, he's a woman."

Mabel Row Curtis writes, "Those good people, sensing Charley's humiliation if confronted with the fact that he was unmasked, never mentioned it to a soul until after Charley's death."

One doctor claimed that at some point in her life, Charlie had been a mother.

Unknowingly, Parkhurst could claim a national first. After voting on Election Day, November 3, 1868, Charlie was probably the first woman to cast a ballot in any election. It wasn't until 52 years later that the right to vote was guaranteed to women by the nineteenth amendment.

Chapter 15

Isadora Duncan

First lady of dance

Isadora Duncan invented what came to be known as Modern Dance. Traditionally, European and American theatrical dance centered on ballet.

Duncan and Ruth St. Denis were the first to break away from classical ballet, using their bodies as instruments to express such emotions as passion, fear, joy, or grief.

Isadora was a thinker as well as a poet, gifted with a lively poetic imagination with a radical defiance of "Things as they are." She had the ability to express her ideas with verve and humor.

Breaking with convention, Isadora traced the art of dance back to its roots as a sacred art. Lori Belilove, founder of the Isadora Duncan Foundation for Contemporary Dance in New York City, said, "Virtually alone, Isadora restored dance to a high place among the arts.

Isadora Duncan

103

Isadora, said Belilove, developed free and natural movements inspired by the Greek arts, folk dances, social dances, nature and natural forces, as well as athleticism which included skipping, running, jumping, leaping, and tossing.

She wore free-flowing costumes, danced with bare feet and loose hair.

Isadora's father was a poet and her mother was a music teacher. Her father supported his family through running a lottery, publishing three newspapers, owning a private art gallery, directing an auction business and owning a bank.

When the bank fell into financial ruin, her father abandoned Isadora's family, and moved to Los Angeles.

After divorcing Isadora's father, Isadora's mother found a small, drab home in Oakland for her brood of four children. They were desperately poor, but the children loved to sing, loved to play-act, and above all, loved to dance.

As a child, her mother instilled in Isadora a love for dance, theater, Shakespeare and reading. The precocious Isadora, even at the age of six, danced for money and taught other children to dance.

Her dance techniques blended poetry, music and the rhythms of nature. Isadora did not believe in the formality of conventional ballet but preferred a more free form of dance.

When Isadora was fourteen, pupils, children of neighbors, came to her to be taught to dance. Her Oakland classes grew and then she held classes across the bay in San Francisco.

Isadora and her sister, Elizabeth, took the ferry-boat each day to San Francisco, and then walked from the Ferry building to Sutter and Van Ness Avenue. They had rented the Castle mansion for a dance studio.

Her first auditions before theatrical directors didn't go well. They watched her dance and told her it was very lovely, but it wasn't the accepted way to dance. It wasn't the way of the theater.

She eventually got an engagement to dance in a music hall in San Francisco. Isadora's Grecian dance and costume did not capture the beer drinking audience in the smoky music hall.

Her luck changed when one night, in the audience, sat theatrical producer Augustin Daly. He saw in Isadora's dance what no others in the audience could see. Daly cast Isadora as one of Titania's dancing fairies in his production of *A Midsummer Night's Dream* in New York.

Borrowing money from any who would lend it, Isadora and her family decided to try Europe. In London, she secured a few engagements, but not enough to feed the hungry stomachs of her family.

It was one night when Isadora and one of her brothers were dancing in their Grecian veils in the small garden of a tiny house in Kensington Gardens that her future changed.

Quite unexpectedly, a beautiful lady came and watched the two as they danced by the light of the stars while their only audience was their own shadows.

The lady that had stood watching them was Mrs. Patrick Campbell, the idol of the London stage. She took them to her home and had them dance for her while she played piano for them. Mrs. Campbell then introduced them to London society.

Life thereafter became busy and hectic and overflowed with triumphs.

Isadora did not believe in marriage, although she had affairs with stage designer Gordon Craig and with Paris Millionaire Eugene Singer. She had a child by each. Both her children were accidentally drowned while with their English governess.

Later, Isadora did marry Russian poet, Sergei Esenin, but the marriage lasted only a short time.

Isadora's death was as tragic as her early life. Her death occurred in an automobile accident in Paris. When she entered a rented car, Isadora was wearing an immense iridescent silk scarf wrapped around her neck, with the ends streaming in long folds.

She asked the driver to take her to her hotel. Neither she nor the driver noticed that one of the loose ends of her scarf had fallen outside the car. The end caught in the rear wheel of the vehicle while the car was going at full speed.

The force dragged Isadora over the side of the car where she hit the cobblestone street. Her body was dragged for several yards before the chauffeur halted.

Doctors summoned to the scene said Isadora Duncan was killed instantly.

Chapter 16

Mary Ellen Pleasant

She challenged society's norms

At birth, Mary Ellen Pleasant had no last name. She said she was the illegitimate child of a Virginia governor's son (John H. Pleasants) and an enslaved Haitian Voodoo priestess. (As used in this context, the word "Voodoo" means spirit, and refers to the religion descended from a number of African cultures.)

Mary Ellen Pleasant

While she won many of her frequent battles against inequities for others, Mary Ellen was never quit able to win the battle for her own good name.

Mary Ellen was born a slave near Augusta, Georgia between 1814 and 1817. According to ships records and confirming testimony, Mary Ellen arrived in San Francisco in 1852 to escape persecution under the Fugitive Slave Law of 1850.

As a child, she was sent to work in the service of a merchant in Nantucket, Massachusetts. She was a precocious child, and according to her final memoir, could recall the entire day's transactions in the general store where she clerked. This was indeed a feat, in that Mary Ellen could neither read nor write.

When her indenture ended in 1841, Mary Ellen married James W. Smith, a wealthy mulatto. While both Mary Ellen and her husband were mulattos, they each could pass as white.

The couple soon became allied with the Underground Railroad, helping slaves escape to freedom by various routes, by mainly on the railroad from Nova Scotia to Virginia (near Harper's Ferry).

James died suddenly. There were some who felt his death came at Mary Ellen's hand. Nevertheless, he left Mary Ellen a wealthy woman.

Pleasant continued her rescue work for the slaves by sneaking onto plantations and soon became a much-hunted rescue worker. Mary Ellen soon became a much-hunted and infamous rescue worker. She fled to New Orleans to hide out with the family of her second husband.

In New Orleans, Mary had the opportunity to study with social-activist Voodoo Queen Mam'zelle, Marie LaVeaux. LaVeaux had invented a way to use Voodoo to aid the disenfranchised, and Mary Ellen wanted to learn it.

The strategy she learned was how to used the secrets of the rich to get aid for the poor, a "model" that would serve her well in San Francisco.

Slavers continued on her trail, and Mary Ellen was forced to head west. She arrived in San Francisco April 7, 1852. The population at the time was about 40,000 people and to serve them there were 700 gambling establishments.

It was not a safe place, with five murders occurring every six days.

The California Fugitive Slave Act stipulated that anyone without freedom papers could be captured and returned to slavery. Mary Ellen took two identities to conceal the fact that she had no papers.

As Mrs. Ellen Smith, she worked as a white boardinghouse steward-cook. As Mrs. Pleasants, she continued her work to help her people escape from slavery.

Working as Mrs. Smith, she was able to get jobs and privileges for "colored" people in San Francisco. She gained the nickname, "The Black City Hall." As Mrs. Pleasants, she used her money to help ex-slaves fight unfair laws and to get lawyers or business in California.

Mary Ellen became an expert capitalist. Her own assets grew and she prospered. But when European emigrants began taking the menial jobs, anti-black sentiment and national depression mounted.

She traveled east again to help John Brown end slavery forever. Their plans involved dangerous ventures. Mary Ellen wrote, "I'd rather be a corpse than a coward."

John Brown was hanged for his efforts, and Mary Ellen narrowly escaped. Back in California, she continued to fight. When the Emancipation Proclamation and the California Right-of-Testimony of 1863, were passed, Mary Ellen openly declared her race.

She orchestrated court battles to challenge the right of testimony, and in 1868, her battle for the right to ride the San Francisco trolleys set a precedent in the California Supreme Court.

Mary Ellen is said to have amassed a fortune of thirty million.

Chapter 17

Lucille Ball

First Lady of Comedy

Her road to stardom wasn't always easy, but Lucille Ball had both gumption and determination. She had decided early in her life that vaudeville was

what she wanted to do.

Yet, her attempts to get into acting school resulted in rude rejections. Acting instructors informed her that she simply had no talent. Undeterred, she entered the John Murray Anderson-Robert Minton acting school in Manhattan at age seventeen.

Lucille Ball

She managed to land a few showgirl parts and got her first modeling jobs. While often frustrated, Lucille later said, "For some reason, I knew that some day I'd make it as an actress."

She went so far as to change her name, willing to try anything to turn the heads of producers. She began telling producers that she was Diane Belmont, from Butte, Montana. She felt this sounded more glamorous than Lucille Ball from upstate New York.

Fate dealt her another blow early in her life. She collapsed while being fitted for a dress. Doctors diagnosed her condition as rheumatoid arthritis. She had to use a wheel chair during the next two years.

Lucille returned to her hometown of Jamestown, New York, where treatment allowed her to recover and pursue the modeling career she had left when becoming ill. Her career got a shot in the arm with her selection as the "Chesterfield Cigarette Girl."

Theatrical agent Silvia Hahlo was seeking a girl for Samuel Goldwyn's "Goldwyn Girls" when she accidentally ran into Lucille, whom she had seen in the Chesterfield ad. She offered her the Goldwyn Girl job.

Her first movie part in Hollywood was as a slave girl in *Roman Scandals*, starring Eddie Cantor. Later, because she was willing to accept "slapstick" roles that other starlets rejected, Lucille got more jobs and never whined about the siphon water or the pies thrown in her face.

Lucille then got a coveted contract with RKO pictures. Her first assignment was a bit part as a model in the Astaire-Rogers film, *Roberta*. That proved to be a lucky break indeed, as it was Ginger Rogers' mother, Lela that then took Lucille under her wing.

Lela was in charge of RKO's Little Theater and often helped aspiring young starlets. She was, according to Lucille, "...the first person to see me as a clown with glamour."

In 1937, Lucille was given a small role in *Stage Door*. Starring Ginger Rogers and Katherine Hepburn, Lucille's part in the production was small, but she capitalized on it. She jumped from bit player to small supporting roles in "A" pictures, and leading roles in "B" pictures.

Lucille came to be known as the "Queen of the B's" as she was cast in film after film.

While filming the movie, *Dance Girl, Dance*, with Maureen O'hara, Lucille met Desi Arnaz. He had just wowed New York audiences while appearing in *Too Many Girls*.

The cast of *Too Many Girls* Broadway show was in Hollywood to do a movie version of the show. Lucille was to be one of the stars.

Desi, Lucille, and the rest of the cast went to the *El Zarape* nightclub. Lucille later said, "I might as well admit here and now I fell in love with Desi what, bang, in five minutes. There was only one thing better than looking at Desi, and that was talking to him."

Vivian Vance and William Frawley were cast as Fred and Ethel Mertz.

Their whirlwind romance was put on hold as Desi returned to New York for an engagement at the Roxy Theater. Finally, Lucille was able to go to New York to do publicity for *Dance Girl, Dance.*

When interviewed at her hotel, she told the press that she and Desi had decided not to get married. That night, however, Desi had made plans for them to elope. They were married the next day at the Byram River Beagle Club in Greenwich, Connecticut, November 30, 1940.

Desi was drafted into the army and the separation nearly resulted in divorce. Their love for each other overcame the petty jealousies and quarrels that had caused the rift between them.

Lucille's career at MGM where she was now under contract, stalled, and Desi's music engagements kept him traveling. She longed to have a baby, but the two were separated so much it seemed impossible. "We'd been married ten years, and been together a year and two months," she later said. "You can't have children that way—you can't have them over the telephone."

While she continued making movies, including *Sorrowful Jones* and *Miss Grant Takes Richmond*, Lucille also worked in a radio show with Richard Denning, called, *"My Favorite Husband."*

CBS wanted to adapt the show to television but they didn't want Desi to play the part of the husband, saying the show would not be believable. Lucille insisted, saying, "My husband is a Cuban conga-player!" She refused to do the show without him.

To prove the public would accept them together as man and wife, Lucille and Desi put together a vaudeville show. They used the writers of the *My Favorite Husband* radio show, along with Desi's band. The show included dance sketches and comedy routines. The public loved them.

Their vaudeville success changed the minds at CBS, and Desi was in for the television version of *My Favorite Husband*." By this time, Lucille found out she was pregnant.

The show was a success from the beginning. They brought in William Frawley and Vivian Vance to play Fred and Ethel Mertz.

Lucy announced she was pregnant a second time. She and Desi and the producer, Jess Oppenheimer, dreamed up a show called *Lucy Goes to the Hospital* to let Lucille's second child be born on the show. Everything went off as scheduled.

On the day that Desiderio Alberto Arnaz IV was born, the television show that had been previously taped was shown on television.

The episode even knocked President Eisenhower's inauguration ceremonies off the front pages and for years, held the record for being the highest rated episode on a TV show.

Eventually, Desi and Lucy purchased RKO, the same studio where Lucy had been "Queen of the B's". Desi was now working 18-hour days running their businesses and it took its toll on their marriage. They were divorced in 1960.

Lucille married Gary Morton, a stand-up comedian in 1961. She decided to reunite with Vivian Vance and do a new television show, *The Lucy Show*.

She eventually bought out Desi's interest in Desilu productions. She continued working hard, making both movies and doing television. She was devastated when she learned that Desi had lost his battle with lung cancer in December 1986.

In 1989, Lucy made a guest appearance at the Academy Awards along with her good friend, Bob Hope. Soon after, she was admitted to Cedars-Sinai Hospital after suffering a stroke.

While Lucy is gone, she is still making people laugh around the world, as the reruns of her shows remain popular and continue to this day.

Chapter 18

Wakano Mukai

Japanese Picture Brides

The first Japanese came to the United States as the result of shipwrecks in the Pacific Ocean in the 1850s. True emigration didn't begin until 1885, when Japan experienced a depression.

There were two main reasons for the large increase in numbers of Japanese in the United States from 2,039 in 1890 to 24,326 ten years later.

As would be natural, the

Buntaro Mukai and his friend, Uehata-san in picture he sent Wakano, asking her to marry him.

men longed for female companionship and the practice of marriage by photograph became a common practice.

Wakano Mukai was one such Japanese Picture Bride. In a translation by her grandson, Wakano recalled her anxiety in meeting her

117

new husband, Buntaro Mukai, whom she had "married by photograph" only a short time before.

"He was living in Salinas, California, and had left Hiroshima several years ago. Buntaro Mukai looked very handsome in the only

Japanese picture brides arrive at
Angel Island immigration station.

photograph I saw of him," she recalled. "He wore a very striking three-piece suit, as did his friend, Ue-hata-san."

These Japanese Picture Brides required
processing at Angel Island.

She continued, "I agreed to marry Buntaro, even though I had never met him in person and he had never written a letter to me. I later learned that he could neither write nor read Japanese."

"I was 16 years old, and there were only a few other Japanese women on the ship bound for America."

Wakano was only one of several Japanese women bound for America. There were also women of Chinese, Korean and Russian extraction on the ship.

"After three weeks at sea, we finally spotted land, and I was surprised to see that we disembarked on an island (Angel Island) instead of in San Francisco. I had to stay on the island for three days for medical tests and interviews."

Then came the day Wakano was to meet her husband. "My heart fluttered like the wings of a cicada," she said.

"Are you Wakano-san?" were his first words to me.

"Yes," I replied, "Buntaro was shorter than I had expected (he was about four-feet-six-inches tall.)"

Wakano received a shock when she saw the shack in which Buntaro was living. It sat on the edge of a strawberry field where he worked as a farm laborer.

"I never could find the three-piece suit he wore in the photograph," Wakano said later. "I guess he borrowed it from someone."

From 1910 to 1935, Wakano and Buntaro had 11 children. They named their last son "Toichi", which means eleven in Japanese.

"We lived in so many towns up and down California during those years. We went wherever crops needed to be harvested." Wakano said the roughest years were 1941-1945 when she was among the Japanese interred at the Salinas Rodeo Grounds while housing was being built for them.

Wakano and Buntaro had a life of many contradictions during this period. One of their sons, Shinichi, volunteered to fight for the United States Army in Italy.

"One day, in August 1945, I received news about the atomic bombing of Hiroshima. Many of my relatives died in the blast," Wakano said.

"At the end of the war, my family moved to Morgan Hill, California, to begin work in the strawberry fields again. We lived in tents for what seemed like an eternity because we had no home to return to after the war.

"In 1848, my seventh son, Masato, went to Okinawa to serve in the United States Army. I remember feeling so proud of him. He was going back to the country of my birth."

Chapter 19

Emma Nevada

Born in a gold mining camp

One of Nevada City's most celebrated personalities was young Emma Wixom. She exhibited tremendous musical talents very early, singing a rendition of the "Star Spangled Banner" at age three.

Emma Nevada

At an early age, she loved going into the meadows and mountains to imitate birds singing.

When her mother died in 1872, Emma's father kept his word to his wife to make the best for Emma.

Dr. Wixom ordered a grand piano that had to be shipped from Boston around Cape Horn by clipper ship and freighted to Sacramento.

Emma played the piano for hours, and she sang in the church.

Dr. Wixom sent her to Mills Seminary (now Mills College) in Oakland. She graduated from Mills College in 1876. While at Mills, she earned the nickname "Mockingbird of Mills" for her renditions of the tune, "Listen to the Mockingbird."

Emma became fluent in several languages, speaking French, Spanish and Italian. After moving to Europe to pursue her singing career, Emma took the stage name of Emma Nevada, in honor of her native city and state.

In Europe she studied under Mathilde Marchesi, a voice teacher with an excellent reputation in Europe.

After three years of hard study Emma debuted under the name Emma Nevada at Her Majesty's theatre in London. Emma was received with enthusiasm and reviewers predicted a brilliant career for her..

She sang in Europe's major opera houses and performed for royalty, including Queen Victoria. Emma Nevada scored many successes, but her greatest was in San Francisco

Emma later married Dr. Raymond Palmer, and the couple established a residence in Paris, where their daughter Mignon was born in 1886.

She trained her daughter in classical music. When she announced her retirement from the stage in 1907, her daughter Mignon made her debut at the Teatro Costanzi in Rome.

Emma turned to teaching singing in London. She died June 20, 1940, in Liverpool, England.

Chapter 20

Sarah Winchester

What lay behind her mysterious house?

Some say Sarah Winchester thought that as long as she built onto her house she would not die. Others believed she was only an eccentric rich woman with more money than good sense, along with a poor sense of building design.

There is no doubt about her wealth. When her husband, William Wirt Winchester died, she inherited $20 million in cash inheritance, along with $1,000 per day income.

On the advice of a friend, Sarah had consulted a medium. The fortuneteller told Sarah that her family was cursed by the

Sarah Winchester-1862

spirits of all those who had been killed by Winchester rifles, which, by the way, were the source of her wealth.

She was further advised to sell her New Haven, Connecticut home and move west. This she did in 1884. She traveled to San Jose, where she found a six-room home under construction. She convinced the owner to sell her the uncompleted home, along with the 162 acres on which it sat.

The house soon grew to include 26 rooms. Eventually, railroad cars were switched onto a nearby siding to bring building materials and imported furnishings to the house.

Winchester Mystery House

Sarah met each morning with her foreman to go over her hand-sketched plans for the day's work. According to one writer, "The plans were often chaotic but showed a real flair for building. Sometimes though, they would not work out the right way, but Sarah always had a quick solution. They would just build another room around an existing one."

Eventually, Sarah's house grew to a height of seven stories. Inside the house, three elevators were installed along with 47 fireplaces. Countless staircases led to nowhere, simply going up and ending at a ceiling.

The number 13 intrigued Sarah Winchester. Nearly all of the windows contained 13 panes of glass;

the walls had 13 panels; the greenhouse had 13 cupolas; many of the wooden floors contained 13 sections; some of the rooms had 13 windows; and every staircase but one had 13 steps.

It is said that Sarah slept in a different room in the house each night.

The exception is a winding staircase with 42 steps, which would normally be enough to take a climber up three stories. In this case, the steps only rise nine feet because each step is only two inches high.

Her house, it is said, had been designed into a maze to confuse and discourage the bad spirits. Her building allowed her to control the spirits who came to the house to avenge all those men killed by Winchester rifles, the source of her wealth.

Sarah had married William Wirt Winchester. In 1857, he took over the assets of a firm that made the "Volcanic Repeater," a rifle that used a lever mechanism to load bullets into the breech.

The company soon developed the "Henry Rifle," which had a tubular magazine under the barrel. It became the true repeating rifle and a favorite among the Northern troops during the Civil War.

Sarah kept 22 carpenters at work, year around, 24-hours a day. For the next 38 years, the building continued, and the house grew in all directions, inside and out. Even though the house was large and spacious, Sarah never entertained guests. Only she and her servants lived in the house.

The house was badly damaged when the great San Francisco earthquake struck in 1906. Sarah was nowhere to be found when her niece and the servants searched the wreckage.

They were unable to hear the faint cries of Sarah from a second-floor bedroom. When at last, the wreckage was cleared from the door of the bedroom, it was feared that Sarah would be dead.

When she was found, she was shaken, but non-the-less stubborn. She insisted that the front thirty rooms of her ninety-room mansion would have to be sealed off and never used again. She claimed the friendly spirits who directed her in building her home had told her that the earthquake was caused by evil spirits who thought she had spent too much time working on those rooms.

Portions of the Winchester house were left in near ruin. The top three stories had collapsed into the gardens and would never be rebuilt.

Sarah moved onto a luxurious barge in the bay off Redwood City for six months while workmen cleared the rubble caused by the earthquake. While the front thirty rooms were closed for good, Sarah moved back in and set the carpenters, pipe fitters and other workmen back to work building her never-ending house.

On September 4, 1922, at the age of 82, Sarah died at some point in her sleep. She left all of her possession to her niece, Frances Marriot, who had been handling most of Sarah's business affairs for some time.

Her wealth, by this time, had depleted considerably. The furnishings, personal belongings and surplus construction and decorative materials were removed and the structure was sold to a group of investors to be used as a tourist attraction.

Even the moving men were confused when they started removing the furniture. It was a house where downstairs leads neither to the cellar nor upstairs to the roof. It was often a complete maze to the workman seeking a way out with the furnishings. The 26,000-square-foot home mansion is now open to visitors.

One room that visitors never see, however, is the wine cellar. It is known that there was one as Sarah and her niece lived well, having fine wines served with their opulent dinners.

When Sarah went to make a wine selection one day, she saw an ominous-appearing black handprint on the wall. The print was probably that of a workman, but Sarah took it as a sign from the spirits that she was to abandon drinking all alcohol. She had the cellar walled up.

Chapter 21

Mrs. F.A. Van Winkle

Her story, as she told it

> *(Author's note: The following story was adapted from the Museum of San Francisco Web Site. Mrs. Van Winkle was one of the first white women married in California. She related the account in her home in San Francisco.)*

"We came to California the same year as the ill-fated Donner party. It started about a month ahead of us, but it kept taking imaginary short cuts and hurrying until it met with frightful disaster.

"My father, who was captain of our train, led his party of about eighty people across trackless plains and mountains for five months, simply with the sun and the stars as guides, and came west almost as straight as the crow flies.

"He believed in moving every day, if only three miles and the result was that all our oxen were in better condition when they arrived in California than when they started.

"Both father and mother were born in Kentucky, but like a good many other Kentuckians of those days, they moved out to Missouri, where we children were born.

"Then father was appointed Indian Agent at Council Bluffs, Iowa, old Colonel Thomas Benton getting him the position. There was no town there then—just the agency buildings. The only white people besides us were the blacksmith and another family. We children grew up there with the Indians as our playmates.

"There were several Indians—Chippewas, Ottawas and Pottawattomies—at the Council Bluffs agency when father was in charge. They were all lazy. They considered it a disgrace to work, and would rather be killed than made to labor. They didn't know any English, and wouldn't talk much in their own language, but as a girl I used to speak Indian.

"One day I read a pamphlet written by a man who had been in California. His name was Hastings, and he was a cousin to Judge Hastings. His description of the beautiful flowers blooming in winter, of the great herds of Spanish cattle in lovely fields, of glorious scenery, and of the ideal climate and blue skies, made me just crazy to move out there, for I thought such a country must be a paradise.

Mother thought so too, but father told us it was a dangerous trip and that Indians might kill all of us on the way. He had been a good ways west, hunting buffalo, and he knew something of the great stretches of plains. But we kept talking about California until father decided to put it to a family vote whether we should go or stay.

"Father went out with Fremont in 1845 to explore the Far Western country. Father came home in time to lead our party, although we had already decided to go anyway.

"So, in May, 1846, we started, I being then 20 years of age. We hadn't been on the way a month—there were no roads or trails—when we were attacked one day by Indians. Five hundred Cherokees swooped down upon us on horseback and surrounded our wagon train.

"They rode around and around us. Father knew how to deal with Indians and after the wagons had been drawn together at the first alarm, he stepped out to parley with them, and offered flour and tobacco. The Indians of those days were simply crazy for flour and tobacco. They would take a little flour and mix it with water and make it into tortillas and pat them lovingly for hours like little flapjacks and then cook them on hot stones.

"Father took out a half barrel of flour and measured it out, a little cupful to each Indian, and he cut plug tobacco up and gave it to them. Then they all smoked the pipe of peace. We knew father simply detested smoking; it made him sick, and we almost laughed to see him puffing away there with all those Indians.

"We were a little afraid of the Sioux Indians, for they were very wild and fierce. But when we encountered them a little while later, father smoked with them and gave them flour and tobacco, too.

"We ran into one herd of about 500 buffalo, and father killed several, but ordinarily he would not permit any delays or turning aside for game. We came steadily along, making about twelve or fourteen miles a day.

"There was no baggage but bedding and provisions. In one wagon drawn by two big oxen we had the bedding, and we used to ride in that. We rode all the way except up the slopes of the Rocky Mountains and the Sierra Nevada. It was awful coming up those mountains. There were great rocks, waist high, that the wheels had to bump over, and it was all the poor oxen could do to drag the lightened loads.

"Altogether our trip was exceptionally fortunate. We made good time, came by the most direct route, had no sickness and lost but one person, a little baby that died after its mother had tried to doctor it herself.

"We were received at Napa by Mr. Yount, who had lived originally in Howard County, Missouri. He was just as glad to see us as if we had been his own family. He owned seven leagues of land there in the Napa valley, had 600 mares and thousands of horses and cattle.

The whole valley was covered with grazing cattle. In those days the only Americans there were the Gregories, the Stewards, the Derbons and a few other families.

"Spanish vaqueros used to be riding all over the country in little groups. They never bothered us or happened in for meals. All they needed was a piece of jerked beef and some roasted corn, and they would carry that with them and ride hundred and hundreds of miles before returning to their homes.

"There were so many thousands of long-horned Spanish cattle in the country that anybody that liked went out and killed a beef when he needed meat, and no one said anything. And it was good beef, too, probably because there was so much excellent grass.

"All the Spanish families had Indian slaves. They never permitted them to walk, but made them go about on the trot all the time. Those Indians made good slaves, excellent. The Spanish vaqueros used to go up to what is now Ukiah and ride in among the Indian rancherias and drive out the boys and girls, leaving the mothers behind and killing the bucks if they offered any resistance.

"Then they would herd the captives down like so many cattle and sell them to the ranchers. About $100 was the standard price. A good girl would bring that, but some sold for as little as $50.

"I bought one Indian girl from a Spaniard for $100, but soon after that another Indian girl and two boys came to my house of their own accord and explained that they had no home and wanted to work.

"The four of them did all my work, washing, ironing, cooking and housecleaning. One of the girls was a splendid nurse. The shameful treatment of the Indians by the Spanish was never equaled by the whites. As Americans settled up the country the enslaving of young Indians naturally stopped.

"We had a Fourth of July celebration near Napa in 1847. It was given by us at the Yount place. It must have been the first affair of the kind in California.

"We had about forty guests, most of them Spanish people of some prominence in the country. I made an enormous pound cake for the center of the table.

"Nobody had brought an American flag to California, so my sister, now Mrs. Wolfskill of Winters, made a little one of some narrow red ribbon and cut some blue silk from her best dress, and sewed on but one star, for material was very scarce, and the whole thing was not bigger than a woman's handkerchief.

"We stuck it in the top of the cake. One of our guests was a Dr. Bailey, an Englishman of whom we all thought a great deal. He died long ago, but his two daughters are married and are living near St. Helena in Napa County, where they own big wine vineyards.

"Father had written across the little flag, 'California is ours as long as the stars remain.' The Spaniards took it all right, but Dr. Bailey became very much excited and snatched at the flag. All through the dinner he insisted upon removing it, declaring that the American flag should never wave over California.

"After the dinner, as my sister and I were driving to our house, Dr. Bailey rode beside our wagon and we clung to the little silk flag and kept waving it at him from one side and then the other as he urged his horse close and tried to grab it from our hands. About a dozen years ago father lent the flag to the California Pioneers, and they have it in their collection yet.

"It used to be claimed that I was the first white woman married in California, but Miss Yount was married in 1845 to Mr. Davis. There were many early Spanish brides just as white skinned as I. Father had moved to San Francisco, now called Benicia, and had started a boarding-house.

"Dr. Semple, who was a native of Kentucky, owned nearly all the land where the town is now. In those days that was thought to be the coming city. The present San Francisco was but an insignificant group of tents occupied by Spanish people and bearing the name Yerba Buena. Governor Vallejo had made Dr. Semple a present of half of Benicia, believing that he would build it up.

136

"I was married in Benicia in the fall of 1847. The ceremony was performed in the big dining room of father's boarding house, which was decorated for the event. There were two other women in town at the time, besides mother and my sisters, and they and about twenty sailors were at my wedding.

"The sailors were as proud as could be and came all dressed in white suits. We gave them a supper affair and they all enjoyed it. The wedding was set for 9 o'clock, but it was a stormy, rainy night, and very dark.

"Ex-Governor Boggs of Missouri was to come visit Napa to perform the ceremony. We waited until 10 o'clock, and were just despairing of seeing him that night when he arrived. He had ridden horseback all the way through mud and water, and he was a very large, stout man, too.

"My husband, Dr. Semple, owned the only ferryboat at Benicia. It was often said that he made money enough with it to sink that boat a half dozen times over, but he was one of the most remarkable speculators I ever knew, and went right through his money.

"Our town was San Francisco, but the people down here took the name away from us. Dr. Semple opposed them, but it did no good. They named this place San Francisco and dropped the name Yerba Buena, so Dr. Semple called his town Benicia, after Mrs. Vallejo, whose maiden name was Francisca Benicia.

"At first we thought California would be a great stock country, a fine place for farming, an elegant climate to live in, but no one had any idea then that there was gold here. But in 1848 and 1849 Dr. Semple

137

was the only man left in Benicia, and mother, my sister and I the only women. All the others had gone to the mines. We lived in Benicia just four years, then we moved to what is now Colusa.

"My husband owned half of Colusa, old Colonel Hagar owning the other half. Dr. Semple had an idea that he could make a fortune out of the land. So we went up there. We were the first white people in that part of the State.

"There was a big rancheria of Indians right in what is now the heart of the town of Colusa, hundreds and hundreds of them. And five miles up the river was another big rancheria on what is now known as the John Boggs place. John Boggs did not come to Colusa until a good deal later, but he had big droves of cattle, and did well and made money.

"In Colusa, in the early days we raised vegetables to sell to the miners, and we grew grain and shipped it down to San Francisco on steamers.

"When I first saw Sacramento it was an apparently endless sweep of small tents, not a frame building anywhere in sight. That was in 1850. It was a terrifying place. I was frightened. Men were gambling on all sides. They were shooting and cursing and yelling. The noise and uproar were awful.

"I lived in Colusa for thirty-two years, never getting away much. It was along in the seventies before I saw San Francisco and I haven't visited Benicia for many years.

"Little by little, as more white people settled in Colusa, the Indians moved back farther from civilization. They disappeared somewhere. I still own a lovely home place of 670 acres at Colusa, and I've been offered $75 an acre for it and wouldn't take it.

"About ten miles from the house is an Indian rancheria, with a little colony of Indians. They sell chickens and pigs, and in the summer time they work in the harvest field and manage to get along pretty well.

"There at Colusa are the graves of my parents—my mother, who died twenty years ago, and my father, who died ten years ago, and there in Colusa lives my nephew, Willard Green, the editor of the Colusa Sun.

"He was the very first white person ever in Colusa. He spent a year there taking care of the property of his uncle, Dr. Semple, before we moved up from Benicia."

Mrs. Susan Cooper Wolfskill of Winters, widow of the late John Wolfskill, who arrived in Los Angeles in 1834, is a sister of Mrs. Van Winkle. She is visiting her younger sister, Mrs. Martha Cooper Roberts, at 564 Fourteenth Street, in Oakland. Mrs. Wolfskill supplements her older sister's reminiscences with some further interesting takes of the very earliest pioneering days.

"I saw the first gold that was discovered in California," said Mrs. Wolfskill. "James Marshall came over to our house in Benicia and stayed all night. He was on his way to San Francisco from Sutter's mill. He said he thought he had gold.

"He took out a little rag that looked like the bit of a bag that housewives keep aniseed in and opened it. We all looked at it in wonder. Three days after that Sam Brannan, a Mormon, came riding breathless into our place in Benicia and asked John Wolfskill, who was afterward my husband, for a fresh horse.

"He said that gold had been discovered, and that he was going up there to locate all the land he could and return to Monterey and file on it. Monterey was then the capital of California.

"But some time before that Brannan had been very unaccommodating to Mr. Wolfskill when he wanted horses to help bring his fruit trees from Los Angeles, so he would not let Brannan have a horse. Brannan rode on, urging his tired beast. He and [John] Bidwell were going to locate the whole gold-bearing country, but Mr. Wolfskill told them it was placer mining, and that they could not hold it all.

"Everybody was guarding the secret of gold in California in hope of monopolizing the product. My father was the first man to write of the discovery. He sent a long letter East to his old friend, Senator Thomas Benton, who had secured him the position of Indian Agent at Council Bluffs years before, and that letter of my father's was primarily the cause of the gold fever that swept through the Eastern States.

"In 1848 and 1849 we had a school in Benicia. Father started it and got seven pupils to come from a distance and board at our place. They were Clements Harbin from Napa, whose family afterward owned Harbin Springs; Nanny Harlin from Martinez, and Lucy, Carmelita, Ellen, Joe and Goyla Knight from Knight's Ferry. The other pupils were my two brothers and myself and my two sisters, Mrs. Calmes, who is now dead, and Mrs. Roberts, now of Oakland.

"In 1849 and 1850 our only source of social amusement was dancing. And such dances! We used to ride horseback miles to attend them. I rode all the way from Benicia to Sonoma, about thirty miles, and then danced all night.

"And the only music for these balls was the fiddle. We left Benicia in 1852 and went to Green valley, and lived there three years. Then we moved to Colusa, and I stayed there until 1860, when I was married and went to Winters to live on the old Wolfskill place, where my husband died."

Chapter 22

Olive Oatman

Captured by Indians as a young girl

When only 15 years old, Olive Oatman was snatched from their covered wagon. Her sister Mary was also taken.

The Oatman family was bound for California. Their parents, Royse and Mary Ann Oatman, were slaughtered in front of the girls, and their wounded brother, Lorenzo, was left for dead.

Their Apache captors held the girls as slaves for a year at a village near Congress, Arizona.

They were then sold to the Mojave Chief Espaniol near Needles, California.

Olive Oatman
Chin tattoos marked
her as an Indian slave.

The Mojave's of the lower Colorado River were unique. They were one of

143

the few tribes that relied on farming, but who were also very warlike.

They were fond of personal adornment. Consequently, the chins of their two young captives were decorated with indelible blue cactus tattoos to mark their status as slaves.

In the 1860s, Olive gave public lectures on the plight of her family and the capture of her and her sister. She described her captives as "filthy, lazy and ignorant." The men especially, she said, were indolent and only when necessity drove them to it would they seek food.

Olive's sister Mary died of starvation during a year of drought. Often fearing death, Olive was made to watch as other Mojave prisoners were tortured. The U.S. Army finally located her and began negotiations for her freedom.

Wearing a bark skirt, and able to speak only halting English, Olive was ransomed at Fort Yuma, Arizona, for a horse, blankets, and beads. She was fortunately reunited with her brother Lorenzo, who had been left for dead.

The Reverend Royal B. Stratton interviewed Olive Oatman and her brother, Lorenzo, for a book within a few months of her return from Indian captivity. The book sold well, and Reverend Stratton used the profits to educate Olive and Lorenzo. They did attend school for a few months in Santa Clara Valley, California.

Olive married John Brant Fairchild in 1865. He burned all copies of Stratton's book that he could lay his hands on. The couple eventually moved to Sherman, Texas, where he was president of the City

Bank. He made a fortune there in banking and real estate.

Chapter 23

Jessie Benton Fremont

She directed her husband's affairs

While Jessie Benton loved her father, she couldn't accept his decision forbidding her to marry John C. Fremont, a noted explorer and mapmaker for the U.S. Army.

Jessie Benton Fremont

Jessie obviously had inherited her father's iron will. While only 17-years-old she eloped with the dashing Fremont, finding herself faced with a totally new life.

"I had never lived out of my father's house, or in any way assumed a separate life from the other children in the family," she said. "I had never been obliged to think for or take care of myself, and now I was to be launched literally on an unknown sea, travel towards an unknown country, everything absolutely new and strange about me, and undefined for the future."

Jessie had been well schooled in politics by her father, Thomas Hart Benton, influential senator from Missouri. While her fathergrudgingly disapproved of her elopement and marriage to John C. Fremont, he eventually came to approve of her choice.

Jessie often accompanied John on his various assignments with the Army. She and her husband wrote a number of best-selling stories of western explorations that made both John Fremont and his scout, Kit Carson, famous.

John Fremont

While John and Jessie were often separated for long periods during the early years of their marriage, Jessie was very instrumental in her husband's progress. She, with his approval, assumed all of his secretarial duties. It was she that took dictation and wrote the flowing reports that gained him promotions in the military.

In 1856, Jessie became the first candidate's wife to play an active part in her husband's presidential campaign. At rallies, where Fremont's name was placed on the slate of candidates, the slogan was "Fremont and Jessie too." While Fremont lost in his presidential attempt, he did get a lot of northern votes.

In 1843, John planned a second expedition, this time to survey and map the Oregon Trail region from the Rocky Mountains to the Pacific. It would be the most important exploring expedition since Lewis and Clark's epic journey nearly 40 years before.

Jessie was able to thwart an order from Secretary of War James Madison Porter. Porter expressed his displeasure with the way Fremont had delayed ordering the howitzer until the last minute, when it would be too late to deny its purchase.

The Secretary of War directed Colonel John J. Abert, of the Topographical Corps, to have Fremont return to Washington. A replacement would be sent to take over his expedition.

John was then at a base four hundred miles from St. Louis, preparing to leave on the expedition, when Jessie intercepted the letter in St. Louis.

As she was told to do by her husband, Jessie opened all mail and carried out all duties that a secretary would.

When she read the letter, she knew it would crush John to be removed from the expedition west.

Jessie hurriedly wrote John a quick note of her own, urging him to start on his journey at once. *"Only trust me and Go!"* she pleaded. She then sent for Baptiste Derosier, a French Canadian voyageur who planned to join John's expedition at the last moment.

The Fremont Flag

Because John Fremont was on a topographical expedition into areas claimed by Mexico, he chose not to carry a regular U.S. flag. Instead, his wife, Jessie, drew and made this flag, using elements from the Stars and Stripes and Army regimental flags.

"How long will you need to get ready?" asked Jessie.

"The time to get my horse," Derosier replied.

In John's return message, he said simply, "I trust, and GO."

Senator Thomas Benton, Jessie's influential father, backed his daughter's action. He himself fired off a letter condemning Fremont's recall. Seven months later, he extracted an even greater revenge.

Wielding his power as chairman of the Committee on Military Affairs, Benton blocked Secretary of War Porter's senate confirmation, forcing him to resign. Jessie was jubilant at the outcome of the confrontation, which had all been inspired by political agendas in the first place.

Later reports note that the letter that Jessie intercepted was much less threatening than she claimed it was. Historians say that the letter did not mention replacing Fremont with another man, as Jessie claimed. Her story, which she repeated both orally and in her writings continued to be embellished somewhat with each telling.

Jessie used her political expertise to make decisions for John. She organized his military campaign so much that her critics called her, "General Jessie". In spite of her help, John seemed always to be in trouble.

In 1848, soon after California gained its independence from Mexico, there was a dispute as to who should be made territorial governor of California. One military commander appointed Fremont to the post.

Another commander, however, did not agree and ordered Fremont to step down. He refused and was ordered back to Washington to face court martial. President Polk pardoned him, but he was no longer Lieutenant Fremont.

Still another incident, which Jessie admits she should have advised against, was John's proclamation to free all Missouri slaves. John hated slavery. His trouble came about because he had neglected to confer with the President before issuing the order.

Lincoln became very angry with him. Jessie, always the protector, went to Washington to see Lincoln. While the President listened to her explanation of John's reasoning, he still removed John Fremont from the command of St. Louis and the Union's Western area.

Unable to be a success in either New York or in California, John declared bankruptcy in 1873.

Jessie started writing books and articles to support the family. She remained faithful to her husband, even when she heard rumors that he was being unfaithful. John died in 1890. Twelve years later, Jessie died.

Chapter 24

Nancy Kelsey

California's First White Woman Emigrant

When Nancy Kelsey was questioned about the arduous journey lying ahead, she steadfastly said, "Where my husband goes I can go. I can better stand the hardships of the journey than the anxieties of an absent husband."

In 1838, at the age of 15, Nancy, the daughter of pioneers, married farmer Ben Kelsey, who is 12 years her senior. Together they eked out a living on a small farm in Missouri.

Nancy Kelsey

The stories of California's gold rush stirred the wanderlust in Ben Kelsey. He had heard so much about the riches and open land in California, that he, his brothers, and members of their families organized a party of ambitious pioneers to make the journey, even though they had no knowledge of the terrain.

In the spring of 1841, a wagon party that included thirty-five men, five women and ten children left the town of Sapling Grove, Missouri, heading for the golden land of California.

John Bidwell, who had migrated to the "Far West", which was then Missouri, organized this unprecedented wagon party for California. The group became known as the Bartleson-Bidwell Company party. John Bartleson had been further west than any other members of the party and was made captain.

It was already late in the season for such a venture to begin, especially in view of the lack of knowledge that anyone in the party had of what lay ahead.

John Bidwell

One man claimed that he had seen a map showing two rivers running out of a great lake all the way to the Pacific Ocean. Find that lake, he told them, and there lays California.

The wagon train turned their teams westward, following the Platte River. All went well until they reached Fort Laramie and the South Pass of the Rocky Mountains. It was there that seven of the men in the party decided they had gone as far west as they wanted to go.

When the wagon train reached Soda Springs, north of Salt Lake, the party split. One group turned toward Oregon, which sounded safer than the route to California. The other group continued toward California.

Ben and Nancy Kelsey, determined to get to California, elected to go with this group. The division of the train left Nancy as the only woman among the 31 men in the wagon party going to California.

The only information the wagon party had was that there was supposed to be a river, called either Mary's River, Ogden's River, or the Humboldt River. Nobody knew exactly what it was called. Worse, yet, nobody had any idea of how to find this river.

It was then believed that the Humboldt River flowed from the Great Salt Lake to the Sacramento River in California. The party began a frantic search for the legendary Humboldt River. Their plan was to follow this eccentric stream to its sink.

One story notes that the travelers were so ignorant of the western geography they faced that some had even brought boat-building equipment. When they reached the Great Salt Lake, they thought they could simply build a boat and float down its outlet to the ocean.

The party sought information at Fort Hall, where some of the men had gone for provisions. The advice they received was as faulty and no better than their own strange notions.

Army officers at Fort Hall could only tell them to be careful not to turn west too soon, or they would become lost and perhaps perish in the canyons and chasms below the Snake River. The soldiers also warned not to go too far south or they might die of thirst in the salty desert.

By August 26, the emigrants were completely lost, but kept moving west. They continued traveling toward a green spot five miles away. Here was a small canyon and both the water and grass were good.

The group rested there for 10 days. Scouts, in the meantime, continued their search for the Humboldt River. On September 9, the scouts came back into camp with word that Mary's River, now called the Humboldt, was only five days away.

Finally, the Kelseys had to abandon their wagon. Nancy continued the journey either on horseback or afoot. They slaughtered the oxen pulling this wagon for food. Ben fashioned packs for the horses to carry food and other necessities, but Ben himself walked from then on.

Finally, the party crossed the 9,000-foot summit of what would later be named the Sonora Pass. Traveling down through a maze of treacherous canyons carved by the Stanislaus River, the emigrants watched dismayed as four of their pack animals fell over a bluff.

Unbeknownst to members of the party, they had already crossed into California territory. One member of the wagon party was sent out as a scout. He returned, saying an Indian had informed him in sign language and broken English that they were not far from the ranch of a white man named Marsh.

Bidwell and his party had completed a 2,000 miles journey, opening the California Trail. Much of this trail would never be used again as quicker and less dangerous routes over the Sierra were found.

Joseph Chiles, traveling with the group, wrote the following about Nancy, the first white woman to ever see Utah:

"Her cheerful nature and kind heart brought many a ray of sunshine through clouds that gathered round a company of so many weary travelers. She bore the fatigue of the journey with so much heroism, patience and kindness that there still exists a warmth in every heart for the mother and child, that were always forming silver linings for every dark cloud that assailed them."

Nancy became the first white woman to reach California in an overland emigrant party. At one time, she was left alone with her baby for about a half-day while the men searched for a way down from the Sierra.

"I was afraid of the Indians. I sat all the while with my baby in my lap on the back of my horse. It seemed to me while I was there alone that the moaning of the winds through the pines was the loneliest sound I had ever heard."

A December entry in her diary noted the following: "In December we went with Sutter in a leaky rowboat to his fort at what is now Sacramento. We were fifteen days making the trip. The boat was manned by Indians, and Sutter instructed them to swim to the shore with me and the child if the boat should capsize. We arrived at the fort on Christmas Day."

157

A week after arriving at Sutter's Fort, Nancy gave birth to a son, who lived only one week.

In 1846, Nancy and her family moved into a cabin in the Napa Valley. There she worked as a seamstress and cook for John C. Fremont's volunteers in the Bear Flag Rebellion.

She and two other women furnished the cloth for the first Bear Flag.

Nancy and Ben were itinerants, never staying in one place for long. In 1856, they headed for Mexico to improve Ben's failing health. While in Mexico, Nancy bore two more children.

Later moving to Texas, Mary Ellen, their now 13-year-old daughter, was captured by Comanche Indians, scalped and raped. The child died in Fresno, California, at age 18, reportedly from the wounds she had suffered earlier.

In later years, Nancy reminisced, "I have enjoyed riches and suffered the pangs of poverty. I saw General Grant when he was little known. I baked bread for General Fremont and talked to Kit Carson. I have run from bear and killed all other kinds of game."

Ben Kelsey died in Los Angeles in 1889 and Nancy moved to a lonely place called Cottonwood Canyon, near Cuyama Valley, about sixty miles east of Santa Maria.

Relatives helped her build a small cabin and she earned her living by raising chickens and by practicing herbal medicine and serving as a mid-wife.

Her final wish, before dying from cancer in 1896, was that she have a real coffin instead of "something scraped together with old board." Friends and relatives saw that her wish was granted.

Chapter 25

Mrs. Bassett

She supplied homesick miners with puppies

Her first name is lost to posterity, but Mrs. Bassett does indeed deserve her place in California history.

Mrs. Bassett arrived in the little village of Butte Mills during the heat of the gold rush. She arrived on foot, with few possessions other than her three dogs—two females and one male. They were all of uncertain ancestry.

When Mrs. Bassett arrived at the west branch of the Feather River, she decided to set up her tent and try her luck at gold panning. While she was said to be a hardy soul, she simply was not a good gold prospector.

She had to make a living, and before long her dogs provided the answer. One of her females had a litter of puppies and an idea was spawned in Mrs. Bassett's head.

The perceptive Mrs. Bassett began selling her puppies to the homesick and companionless gold miners for a pinch of gold dust for each.

Soon, every cabin and tent in the area had a canine companion. Not only miners, but storeowners, saloonkeepers and other residents of the area soon had a dog or two.

There were only ten houses in the entire village, but the town had sixteen dogs. The origin of the dogs goes back to the arrival of Mrs. Bassett, for before she arrived, there were no dogs at all.

Strangers arriving in town often remarked, "This must be Dogtown!"

The name stuck. (The "Dogtown" in Butte County is not to be confused with a "Dogtown" in Mono County.)

Until 1859, Dogtown was not widely known nor highly populated, something the local residents preferred. The community gained wide fame soon after, however, when a 54-pound gold nugget was found on the slopes of Sawmill Peak.

A.K. Stearns, a workman, found the gold nugget in the Willard Claim, a hydraulic mine owned by three miners whose names were Willard, Wetherbee, and Smith. The nugget was valued at $10,690. At today's prices, estimates put the value of the nugget at more than $350,000. Reports claim a 96-ounce nugget was found on the same site in 1854.

This rich piece of ore was dubbed the "Dogtown Nugget" and made the headlines of newspapers across the United States. The news started a small gold rush of its own to the Dogtown area.

While "Dogtown" may have suited the men just fine as a name, the women didn't appreciate their town's name one bit. They resented having to write "Dogtown" on their letters to family and friends back home. It should be noted that it cost two dollars for postage to send a letter from Marysville to Dogtown and took up to three weeks for delivery.

On August 16, 1860, The *Marysville Appeal* ran a letter from one of the discontented wives living in Dogtown.

"We should hate to live in a place called 'Dogtown', particularly if we had a large correspondence and had to write the name frequently."

The women of Dogtown waged a strong campaign to change the name. After much discussion, Dogtown was renamed "Magalia", the Latin word for "cottages". The Magalia name was apparently adopted for the Magalia mine that was discovered in the area in 1855.

Large-scale mining continued in Dogtown or "Magalia" until the 1890s.

(This story was adapted from one appearing in "The Dogtown Territorial Quarterly, now known as The California Territorial Quarterly)

Chapter 26

'Biddy' Mason

This black slave gained prominence in L.A.

Bridgett "Biddy" Mason grew up as a slave in Mississippi on a plantation owned by Robert Marion Smith. She gave birth to three daughters, all fathered by her owner, Robert Smith.

Biddy was born in the year 1818. On the plantation where she grew up, slaves were common property and Biddy served as a slave for thirty-eight years.

Biddy Mason

Robert Smith, became a Mormon convert in 1847, and decided to move his household and his slaves to Utah Territory to help build the Kingdom of the Saints in Salt Lake City.

It was Biddy's job to herd the cattle, prepare meals, and take care of the children on the two thousand mile trek. When Brigham Young then decided to open a Mormon Colony in San Bernardino in 1851, Smith again decided to move.

At the time of his move to California, Smith apparently was unaware of the fact that the California's state constitution forbade owning of slaves.

After learning of this, Smith made plans to move to Texas, which was still a slave state. Biddy Mason did not want to travel to Texas and remain a slave. She petitioned the court to grant her freedom from her owner.

A court date was scheduled. Slave owner Robert Smith did not appear in court. Therefore, Biddy Mason's petition for manumission (*the process of emancipation from slavery*) was granted. She and other members of her family were all freed.

Judge Benjamin Hayes also granted freedom for ten other Afro-American women and children, all of whom had been held as slaves by Robert Smith.

Fortunately for Biddy and her daughters, this was a year before the Dred Scott decision that allowed slaves to be taken to free states without their status changing. Otherwise, it is doubtful that Judge Hayes would have ruled in their favor.

During the petitioning process, Mason and her children had moved into the home of Charles Owens, who assisted her in obtaining her freedom. One of her daughters later married Owens and had two children.

In 1884, Mason bought a commercial building on Spring Street and rented out office spaces. She told her

166

daughters to never let go of the Spring Street property. Her intuitiveness proved correct, for the piece of land that Biddy Mason purchased is now in the center of Los Angeles' commercial district. She acquired several other prime properties and from the money she earned, she was able to educate her children. Her descendants prospered and one of her grandsons, Robert, became a successful politician and real estate developer. He was one of the richest African American men in Los Angeles.

Mason was very generous and participated in many charitable activities in her community. She visited jails and provided financial assistance to people of all races. She established a day-care center and a nursery for working parents. She was very religious and in 1872, helped found the Los Angeles branch of the First African Methodist Episcopal Church.

Biddy Mason was never selfish with her money, giving generously to various charities as well as providing food and shelter to the poor of all races. There were often lines of needy people at 331 South Spring Street.

Biddy died on January 15, 1891 and was buried in an unmarked grave at Evergreen cemetery in Los Angeles. Ninety-seven years later, in 1988, Los Angeles Mayor Tom Bradley and other members of the First African Methodist Episcopal Church unveiled a tombstone to mark her grave.

November 16, 1989 was declared Biddy Mason Day in Los Angeles and a memorial depicting her life and achievements was unveiled at the Broadway Center multipurpose building.

About the Author

Alton Pryor has been a writer for magazines, news-papers, and wire services for more than 35 years. He worked for United Press International in their Sacramento Bureau, handling both printed press as well as radio news.

He then journeyed to Salinas, where he worked for the Salinas Californian daily newspaper for five years.

In 1963, he joined California Farmer magazine where he worked as a field editor for 27 years.

When that magazine was sold, the new owners forced him into retirement, which did not suit him at all. He then turned to writing books. He is a gradu-ate of California State Polytechnic University, San Luis Obispo, where he earned a Bachelor of Science degree in journalism.

Index

171